COMPACT *Research*

Deforestation

by Lydia Bjornlund

Energy and the Environment

ReferencePoint
Press®

San Diego, CA

About the Author

Lydia Bjornlund is a freelance writer in northern Virginia, where she lives with her husband, Gerry Hoetmer, and their children, Jake and Sophia. She has written more than a dozen books for children and young adults. She also writes books and training materials on land conservation, public management, and industrial design for adult audiences. Bjornlund holds a master's degree in education from Harvard University and a BA from Williams College.

For more information, contact:
ReferencePoint Press, Inc.
PO Box 27779
San Diego, CA 92198
www. ReferencePointPress.com

Picture credits:
Cover: iStockphoto.com
iStockphoto.com: 13, 16
Steve Zmina: 31–33, 46–49, 62–64, 76–79

LIBRARY OF CONGRESS CATALOGING-IN-PUBLICATION DATA

Bjornlund, Lydia D.
   Deforestation / by Lydia Bjornlund.
     p. cm.
   Includes bibliographical references and index.
   ISBN-13: 978-1-60152-075-3 (hardcover)
   ISBN-10: 1-60152-075-1 (hardcover)
   1. Deforestation—Juvenile literature. I. Title.
   SD418.B35   2008
   333.75'137—dc22

                             2008054558

Contents

Foreword

"Where is the knowledge we have lost in information?"

—T.S. Eliot, "The Rock."

As modern civilization continues to evolve, its ability to create, store, distribute, and access information expands exponentially. The explosion of information from all media continues to increase at a phenomenal rate. By 2020 some experts predict the worldwide information base will double every 73 days. While access to diverse sources of information and perspectives is paramount to any democratic society, information alone cannot help people gain knowledge and understanding. Information must be organized and presented clearly and succinctly in order to be understood. The challenge in the digital age becomes not the creation of information, but how best to sort, organize, enhance, and present information.

ReferencePoint Press developed the *Compact Research* series with this challenge of the information age in mind. More than any other subject area today, researching current issues can yield vast, diverse, and unqualified information that can be intimidating and overwhelming for even the most advanced and motivated researcher. The *Compact Research* series offers a compact, relevant, intelligent, and conveniently organized collection of information covering a variety of current topics ranging from illegal immigration and deforestation to diseases such as anorexia and meningitis.

The series focuses on three types of information: objective single-author narratives, opinion-based primary source quotations, and facts and statistics. The clearly written objective narratives provide context and reliable background information. Primary source quotes are carefully selected and cited, exposing the reader to differing points of view. And facts and statistics sections aid the reader in evaluating perspectives. Presenting these key types of information creates a richer, more balanced learning experience.

For better understanding and convenience, the series enhances information by organizing it into narrower topics and adding design features that make it easy for a reader to identify desired content. For example, in *Compact Research: Illegal Immigration*, a chapter covering the economic impact of illegal immigration has an objective narrative explaining the various ways the economy is impacted, a balanced section of numerous primary source quotes on the topic, followed by facts and full-color illustrations to encourage evaluation of contrasting perspectives.

The ancient Roman philosopher Lucius Annaeus Seneca wrote, "It is quality rather than quantity that matters." More than just a collection of content, the *Compact Research* series is simply committed to creating, finding, organizing, and presenting the most relevant and appropriate amount of information on a current topic in a user-friendly style that invites, intrigues, and fosters understanding.

Deforestation at a Glance

President Barack Obama's Energy Agenda

In February 2009, President Obama signed the American Recovery and Reinvestment Act, a $787 billion economic stimulus bill that includes money aimed at doubling the amount of renewable energy produced over 3 years. Additionally, the Obama administration's "New Energy for America" plan sets out long-term policy and spending goals for making the United States a leader on climate change. Many experts say that climate change threatens forests, and that deforestation adds to global warming. The how, what, and when of such spending has prompted considerable debate.

Forests Today

The world has almost 10 billion acres (3.9 billion ha) of forest, covering about 30 percent of the world's land area. Roughly 36 percent of these forests are categorized as primary forests.

Deforestation Today

More than 80 percent of the Earth's natural forests have already been destroyed.

Deforestation Numbers

Today's deforestation rate is about 32 million acres (13 million ha) per year. Accounting for forest area offset by forest planting and natural forest growth, the net rate of loss is about 18 million acres (7.3 million ha) per year.

Changes in Deforestation Rates

The rate of deforestation is slowing. The net rate of loss—the difference between the amount of forest lost and that gained—from 2000 to 2005 was 18 million acres (7.3 million ha) per year, compared with 23 million acres (8.9 million ha) per year from 1990 to 1999.

Where Deforestation Is Occurring

Africa has the highest rate of deforestation of any continent. It lost more than 9 percent of its forest area from 1990 to 2005. Indonesia lost 13 percent of its forest area from 2000 to 2005; Mexico lost 6 percent; Papua New Guinea lost 5 percent; and Brazil, 4 percent during this time.

Ownership

Governments own 84 percent of the world's forests, but private owner-ship is increasing.

Plantation Forests

About 6.9 million acres (2.8 million ha) of forest is being planted per year. About 3.8 percent of the world's total forest area is planted. Productive plantations, established primarily for wood and fiber production, account for 78 percent of the plantation forests; protective plantations, established primarily for soil and water conservation, make up 22 percent.

Wood Production

Production of wood and nonwood forest products is the primary func-tion for 34 percent of the world's forests. More than half of all forests are used for production in combination with other functions.

Overview

"If a considered political decision is to be made about how much forest we want to have in the world, it is crucial for us to have a comprehensive view of the arguments for and against the exploitation of the forests."

—Bjørn Lomborg, environmental author.

"A decade ago, 'saving the rainforest' was something that many acknowledged we *should* do. Now that we have undeniable evidence of the connection between forests, climate and conflict, it is clear this is something we *must* do."

—Jeff Horowitz, founding partner of Avoided Deforestation Partners, a project of the Center for International Politics.

Forests form some of the most important ecosystems on Earth. They provide habitat for millions of animal and plant species and homes for millions of people. Forests are a rich source of food and provide raw materials for the buildings we live in and the medicines that save us from disease. Even in cities, the air and water are cleaned by trees. Forests help maintain a temperate climate and protect us from global warming.

Types of Forests

There are three main types of forests: boreal, temperate, and tropical. Boreal forests form an almost continuous belt around the Earth, stretching across Canada, Russia, Norway, Finland, and Sweden. Until recently, boreal forests have been little changed by humans.

Overview

8

Temperate forests are found in areas with relatively mild weather conditions. The temperate rain forests along the northwest coast of North America are home to some of the Earth's oldest and largest trees, including the Douglas fir, which can grow to 300 feet (91m) high, and California's redwoods, which can weigh as much as 6,000 tons (5,357 metric tons). Most studies suggest that temperate forests—most of which are in North America, Europe, and Russia—are experiencing slow growth.

Tropical forests, which are between the tropics of Capricorn and Cancer, cover approximately 14 percent of the Earth's land surface. There are two main kinds of tropical forests: tropical rain forests and tropical dry forests. Tropical rain forests are the most complex and diverse

> **Forests form some of the most important ecosystems on Earth.**

ecosystems on Earth. Tropical dry forests do not have as many species as rain forests, but they provide habitat for some large, rare species, such as elephants, rhinoceroses, and lions. Much of today's deforestation is taking place in tropical forests.

Forest Classifications

Categorizing forests according to the age and structure of their trees is useful in determining the level of deforestation. A forest that has never been cut is called an old-growth forest—classified by the Food and Agriculture Organization of the United Nations (FAO) as a primary forest. Because old-growth forests have not been disturbed for hundreds of years, they provide untouched habitats for myriad species. Not surprisingly, the deforestation of old-growth forests is of primary concern to environmentalists.

Second-growth forests are those in which logging or other land uses have depleted the forest of some of its original growth and in which new trees have grown in their place. A third type of forest—the plantation forest—consists of trees that have been planted and managed, usually for harvest. In North America, plantation forests are a main source of Christmas trees, for instance; in Southeast Asia, old-growth forests are being cleared to make way for plantations of palm oil trees.

What Is Deforestation?

Put simply, deforestation is the clearing of large forested areas. Deforestation occurs when forestlands are converted for agriculture, ranching, or new residential or commercial development. Deforestation also results from over-harvesting trees for wood or other forest products. Nonhuman impacts, such as fire or other natural disaster, can also contribute to deforestation.

The FAO, a leading source of information on the world's forests, defines deforestation as "the conversion of forest to another land use or the long-term reduction of the tree canopy cover below the minimum 10 percent threshold," which is the amount of tree cover the FAO uses to define a forest.[1] Lesser impacts to a forest are considered forest degradation. The FAO's definition of deforestation includes forestlands that have been converted for farming, pasture, reservoirs, and urban areas but excludes areas where the trees have been removed for harvest or where they are expected to regrow.

The Limitations of Deforestation Data

Although the FAO is widely accepted as the most authoritative source of deforestation data, some environmentalists believe the FAO's definition fails to assess accurately the extent of deforestation. The World Rainforest Movement calls the definition "so broad that most green urban areas can be considered major forest ecosystems."[2] The FAO's definition also limits deforestation to human impacts, ignoring the loss to forest fires and other natural disasters.

Ten thousand years ago, forests covered roughly half the Earth's land surface.

There are also limitations to the technology used to measure deforestation. NASA's Landsat satellite, for instance, measures forest canopy and cannot detect whether the trees and plants have been cleared below it. "The consensus is that Africa is losing about 0.4 to 0.7 percent of its forests each year but this is likely an underestimate," explains Holly Gibbs, who studied the issue as a doctoral candidate. "If you have rain over an open woodland forest, common to parts of Africa, it will 'green up' or sprout flowers. If the satellite takes its image at that time it can have the impression that there is more forest as a result."[3]

Scientists say that it is critical to look behind the amount of forest gained or lost. Asia has experienced a net increase in forest area, for example, but this is due almost exclusively to the planting of trees in China, while deforestation in other Asian countries has escalated. Environmentalists also warn that such plantation forests do not provide the same ecological benefits as forests in which trees have grown over centuries.

How Serious Is Deforestation?

Ten thousand years ago, forests covered roughly half the Earth's land surface. The World Resources Institute estimates that only about 22 percent of this original forest cover remains intact, mostly in three large areas: the Canadian and Alaskan boreal forest, the boreal forest of Russia, and the tropical forest of the Amazon basin. Experts indicate that Russia, Brazil, the United States, Canada, and China together have more than 50 percent of the world's forest.

People have been clearing forests throughout history, making way for farms and settlements and drawing on the rich resources found in wooded areas. In recent decades, however, forests are disappearing at a rapidly increasing rate. A recent study undertaken by the FAO shows that the rate of global deforestation has doubled since 1980. Today an estimated 213,000 acres (86,000 ha) of forest—an area larger than New York City—are lost every day.

Forests at Risk

Until recently, most of the deforestation occurred in Europe, North Africa, and the Middle East; by the turn of the twentieth century, most of the large forests in these areas had lost much of their tree cover. The eastern United States was stripped of its original old-growth forests by 1920, replaced by newer, second-growth forests.

In the last few decades, most deforestation has occurred in the tropics. Tropical forests once occupied 6.2 million square miles (16 million sq. km); today only about 3.5 million square miles (9 million sq. km) remain. Africa has lost more than half of its original forest; Latin America and Asia have lost 40 percent. The removal of tropical forests in Latin America and in Asia is proceeding at a pace of about 2 percent per year. Brazil, which harbors the largest rain forest in the world, also has the highest annual rate of deforestation. Between 1990 and 2005, Brazil lost

163,436 square miles of forest (423,297 sq. km), an area roughly the size of California.

Not everyone agrees with the dire predictions of environmentalists, however. "Globally, forest cover has remained remarkably stable over the second half of the twentieth century,"[4] writes Bjørn Lomborg in his 2001 book *The Skeptical Environmentalist*. Philip Stott, a professor of biogeography at London University's School of Oriental and African Studies and editor of the *Journal of Biogeography*, argues that the deforestation rates touted by conservationists are much too high. "If the rainforest in . . . [the Amazon River basin] was being destroyed at the rate critics say, it would have all vanished ages ago,"[5] he says.

What Causes Deforestation?

The many causes of deforestation are interrelated and vary from one region to another. In many places, deforestation occurs because of logging or the conversion of forested land for cattle ranching and farming. In addition, as urban areas expand outward, land is often converted for housing and commercial and industrial centers. Mining, oil or gas extraction, and development projects may also impact forests.

> With deforestation, water tables fall, land once buffered by woodland becomes more prone to drought, and landslides and flash floods destroy roads, crops, and entire communities.

Local, national, and international political and economic factors play a role in deforestation. Some forests become victims of civil war or conflicts between competing groups. War-torn Afghanistan faces a particularly acute forest loss today. About 70 percent of the country's forests have been cleared during 2 decades of war and internal strife. Similarly, El Salvador has lost 70 to 85 percent of its rain forest due to heavy bombing during the civil war that raged in the mid-1980s. In some places the illegal harvesting and sale of trees and other forest products fund arms and ammunition for rebel forces. In a 2008 article for the *New Yorker*, Raffi Khatchadourian explains the link between illegal logging and fighting:

This truck transports logs from the forest where they were cut down to a processing plant. More than 80 percent of the Earth's natural forests have already been destroyed.

"In 2001, experts with the United Nations in the Democratic Republic of Congo coined a phrase, 'conflict timber,' to describe how logging had become interwoven with the fighting there. . . . In Burma, stolen timber helps support the junta and the rebels. In Cambodia, it helped fund the Khmer Rouge, one of the most brutal rebel factions in history."[6]

Economic globalization is blamed for much of the increase in deforestation, particularly of the tropical forests in developing countries. Poor countries with expanding populations, inequitable distribution of wealth, and corrupt systems of government are especially vulnerable. Poor people often have few options for making income, and they clear the land for agriculture and sell the timber for profit.

What Are the Consequences of Deforestation?

Although the exact number is hard to determine, experts estimate that there may be as many as 150 million indigenous people living in or near forests worldwide, and deforestation may threaten their very existence. "As industrial logging and other developments such as mining and road building move further and further into remaining forests, many of these indigenous peoples' cultures and livelihoods are becoming threatened," says the environmental organization Greenpeace. "Indeed, many cultures have already been lost."[7]

With deforestation, water tables fall, land once buffered by woodland becomes more prone to drought, and landslides and flash floods destroy roads, crops, and entire communities. Deforestation also has been blamed for contributing to global climate changes that affect countries thousands of miles away.

Forest Resources

Throughout the world, wood from forests continues to provide people with fuel for warmth and cooking. Logs are also turned into building materials, furniture, and plywood. Wood pulp is made into cardboard and paper.

But wood is just one of many resources provided by the world's forests. The bark from some types of trees is made into cork; the fibers from others are used for rattan and burlap. Dyes, rubbers, gums, spices, latexes, perfumes, resins, and medicines are among the many forest products on which the world has come to depend.

> "The ingredients for many modern medicines are taken directly from forest plants or trees.

Forests also help to feed the world's population. There are over 100,000 plant species in tropical rain forests around the globe, providing coffee, bananas, chocolate, nuts, fruits, and many other widely popular goods. In addition, the ingredients for many modern medicines are taken directly from forest plants or trees. According to an estimate from the World Health Organization, 80 percent of the people in developing countries rely on traditional medicines for primary health care needs, of which plant extracts are an integral part. Even in the United States, where synthetics dominate the market, plant products are an important part of pharmaceutical drugs; an estimated one-quarter of the drugs prescribed today have plant products as a major ingredient.

Flora and Fauna

Forests provide habitat for a multitude of animals. Scientists estimate that forests contain more than 70 percent of the animal and plant species on Earth. Tropical rain forests, which cover just 7 percent of the Earth's land surface, contain more than half of all the plant and animal species in the world. Many species are so specialized that they can only be found in small areas where a unique set of ecological conditions exist. Their specialization makes them vulnerable to extinction. For example, a rare periwinkle that forms the basis for two widely prescribed cancer drugs has only been found in Madagascar. The loss of Madagascar's forests has led to the periwinkle's extinction in the wild. Many of the world's most endangered and exotic animals depend on the forests for their survival.

> " Governments at all levels are involved in halting the loss of the world's forests by passing and enforcing forest preservation policies and laws. "

In addition to the loss of critical habitat, clearing forestlands increases fragmentation. Areas that were once at the center of the forest are now at its edge. Because a forest's interior is far different from its edges, the so-called edge effect creates problems for forest plants and animals. In a tropical rain forest, for example, the edges are drier and are buffeted by hot winds. Mature trees standing at the margins often die. The edge effect changes the types of trees, plants, and insects that can survive there, increasing the rate of extinction and reducing biodiversity.

Impact on the Environment

Forests have been compared to huge sponges: They soak up rainfall and release it slowly. Forested areas help to reduce the amount of storm water runoff and its impact. The tree canopy in forests captures the rainfall,

This aerial photograph shows a deforested area of the Amazon rain forest in Brazil. The land was cleared to plant soybeans. Between 1990 and 2005, Brazil lost 163,436 square miles of forest, an area roughly the size of California.

giving it more time to evaporate directly into the air rather than adding to the water flowing over the ground. Tree leaves also slow the speed of precipitation, reducing its impact, which in turn reduces soil erosion. Tree roots make spaces in the soil for water to soak in as well as absorbing water from the soil. This makes the soil drier and more stable, so it in turn can support the trees and plants that grow there and keep them from being washed away. Forests store water, replenishing underground water supplies and releasing the water into streams throughout the year, thereby reducing the risk of drought.

Scientists also believe that deforestation contributes to desertification—the process by which land becomes so dry that no vegetation can grow. In a 1980 report, the United Nations Environment Programme estimated that 35 percent of the world's land surface was at risk for desertification and that this could affect 20 percent of the world's population.

How Can Deforestation Be Stopped?

Numerous proposals to stop deforestation have been made by government agencies, private and nonprofit organizations, and individuals. Many focus on national policies and development strategies. Governments at all levels are involved in halting the loss of the world's forests by passing and enforcing forest preservation policies and laws.

The effort cannot succeed without integrating the needs of the local population. Initiatives at the local level are needed to help local populations appreciate the value of forests and encourage them to employ sustainable practices. "Regardless of the international and national policies in place, deforestation cannot be combated effectively unless local landowners and residents have more reason to protect forest ecosystems than they have to destroy them," stresses a coalition of groups called the Avoided Deforestation Partners. "Local communities must have significant input if policies are to succeed."[8]

On a local scale, governments and nonprofit forest conservation organizations work to educate people and organizations about the importance of low-impact agricultural activities and sustainable harvesting of wood and nonwood forest products such as rubber, cork, and medicinal plants. Many governments and private organizations also offer incentives for sustainable land-use practices in and near forested areas—a step that is particularly important in poorer areas where people depend on the forests to make a living.

The Global Nature of the Problem

In general there is less deforestation taking place in industrialized countries than in poorer countries. In part this is because many of the old-growth forests in Europe and North America have already been cleared. Forest management policies of wealthier countries also likely play a role. Perhaps the biggest factor in this disparity is that the market for wood and wood products has become global. Industrialized countries import an increasing amount of lumber and other forest products from developing countries, which become dependent on these exports. Forest cover is increasing in Japan, for example, yet Japan imports more tropical lumber than the rest of the world combined.

Many experts emphasize that success in stopping deforestation depends on recognizing and appreciating the complex causes of deforestation, including the dependence of many poor countries on the income from the sale of forest products. NASA researcher Rebecca Lindsey is among those who suggest making "direct payments to tropical countries for the ecosystem services that intact tropical forests provide."[9]

Many people stress the need for an international response that includes sanctions and financial support for developing countries exporting these products. The United Nations Environment Programme has worked for many years to bring together countries to address issues such as deforestation on a global scale. The World Bank uses loans to reduce poverty in developing countries and to help foster improvements in biodiversity, environmental policies, and land management.

The Role of Private Organizations and Individuals

Wood production and timber companies have a vested interest in protecting forests: Without forests, they would have no source of income. These businesses practice a wide range of forest management techniques, including selective cutting that leaves mature trees in place, tree rotation that allows second-growth forests to grow, and planting new trees. Although forest plantations do not provide the same level of services as old-growth forests, they can provide a means for growing and harvesting wood to meet the world's demand for timber and other wood products. Downstream businesses, such as the pulp and paper industry, can play a critical role by purchasing products only from companies that engage in sustainable practices.

Many private organizations are working to address deforestation. The Nature Conservancy, Community Forestry International, the WWF (World Wildlife Fund in the United States and the Worldwide Fund for Nature in all other countries), and Conservation International are among the many organizations working on a global scale to preserve forest resources and habitats. Some conservation organizations protect forests by purchasing large tracts of land.

Perhaps one of the most important roles that these organizations play is to educate others about deforestation and ways they can help. There are many things the average consumer can do, from reducing the amount of hardwoods used, to buying paper products with recycled content, to boycotting rain forest goods grown unsustainably. The first step is to educate oneself about the causes and effects of deforestation.

How Serious Is Deforestation?

> **This is a super crisis that we are facing, it's an appalling crisis, it's one of the worst crises since we came out of our caves 10,000 years ago. I'm referring of course to elimination of tropical forests and of their millions of species.**
>
> —Norman Myers, a biologist with expertise in deforestation and mass extinction of species.

> **European forest area is constantly growing; North America's forests are not disappearing. In reality, there is about the same amount of forest cover today as there was 100 years ago.**
>
> —Advisory Committee on Paper and Wood Products.

According to the World Resources Institute, more than 80 percent of the natural forests that once blanketed the Earth are gone. Some environmentalists say that high deforestation rates today threaten much of the forest that remains. According to the 2005 Millennium Ecosystem Assessment, a research program that measures ecosystem changes over the course of decades, humans are making more changes to the natural ecosystems today than in any other period in human history. The National Geographic Web site calls deforestation a "modern day plague"[10] and warns that the world's rain forests could completely vanish in 100 years at the current rate of deforestation.

In 2005 the world's total forest area was estimated at 9,766 million acres (3,952 million ha), or about 30 percent of the land area. This corresponds to an average of 1.53 acres (0.62 ha) per capita. The area of forest is unevenly distributed. More than two-thirds of forested land is in just 10 countries, led by Brazil, Russia, and Canada. Seven countries have no forest at all; an additional 57 have forest on less than 10 percent of their total land area.

> " Forests in industrialized countries tend to fare better than in developing countries. "

Most of the forests that still exist have been modified to some degree. According to FAO's 2005 data, only 36 percent of forest area can be classified as primary forests, defined by the FAO as "forests of native species where there are no clearly visible indications of human activities and where the ecological processes are not significantly disturbed."[11] Plantation forests—while growing in number—account for less than 5 percent of the world's forests. Plantations that are planted to harvest wood and fiber account for 78 percent of these forests; protective plantations, which are established primarily for the conservation of soil and water, account for the other 22 percent.

Deforestation Rates

From 2000 to 2005, an average of more than 32 million acres (13 million ha) were cleared each year. Although forests continue to be cleared at what the FAO calls "an alarmingly high rate,"[12] forest planting and restoration have reduced the net loss—that is, the amount of forest cleared minus the forest that has been planted or grown back naturally. Furthermore, the data that have been collected over the past several decades suggest that the overall rate of deforestation is declining. From 1990 to 2000, the world was losing an average of 22 million acres (8.9 million ha) annually; in the first 5 years of the twenty-first century, this rate had slowed to 18 million acres (7.3 million ha)—an area about the size of Panama.

Where Is Deforestation Occurring?

The rate of deforestation varies widely by region—and sometimes by country. The highest rates of deforestation today are in Africa, Latin America, and the Caribbean, where high poverty rates contribute to the deforestation of once lush forests. In many of the countries in these areas, people have few alternatives to using forest resources for food and fuel, and poor people migrate to forestlands and clear them to grow crops. Tropical forests may be at particular risk. When compared with the 1990s, the annual deforestation rate of tropical forests increased in the first few years of the twenty-first century.

Forests in industrialized countries tend to fare better than in developing countries. A 2007 analysis of deforestation trends undertaken by the FAO showed that most countries in Europe and North America are actually showing a net increase in forest area, mostly due to plantation forests. Recent FAO data also show increases in primary forest area in several European countries and Japan.

Deforestation in the Tropics

The loss of tropical forests is of particular concern to many environmentalists. Scientists estimate that there were once 3.7 to 4 billion acres (1.5 to 1.6 billion ha) of tropical forestland; today there is less than 2 billion acres (800 million ha). Brazil and Indonesia—both among the 10 countries with the most forested area—have the greatest loss of tropical forestland. The rate of deforestation in Latin America also appears to be accelerating: The annual rate in the 1990s was 0.46 percent; between 2000 and 2005, the annual rate had risen to 0.51 percent. Some environmentalists warn that unless action is taken, there will be no large areas of tropical forest left in 2025 except for a few patches in the Amazon River valley in Brazil, and in Zaire and New Guinea.

Many countries in Southeast Asia and Africa have less than 10 percent of their original rain forests left. An estimated 95 percent of the rain forest that once covered Madagascar has been destroyed. A century ago, lush forests covered about 80 percent of the Philippines. Today the Philippines has fewer trees per person than any other

> " Some environmentalists warn that unless action is taken, there will be no large areas of tropical forest left in 2025 except for a few patches in the Amazon River valley in Brazil, and in Zaire and New Guinea. "

Southeast Asian country, mostly because of illegal logging.

Still, some experts are optimistic. A 2006 study undertaken by the Smithsonian Tropical Research Institute suggests that deforestation rates will decrease as the rate of population growth slows. "Despite many caveats," write the report's authors, "our projections for forest cover provide hope that many tropical forest species will be able to survive the current wave of deforestation and human population growth."[13]

Although their loss is sometimes overlooked because they are smaller in size than other types of forests, mangrove forests are among the most severely threatened forests in the world. Mangroves line one-quarter of the world's tropical coasts. Many of the mangroves once found along the coasts of Southeast Asia have been removed to make way for large commercial shrimp ponds. Since 1950 Thailand has lost more than half and the Philippines more than three-quarters of the mangroves that once lined their coasts, often with devastating results. The intertwined roots of mangroves shield the land from wind and waves. Stripping the coast of this protection increases the force of storms moving in from the sea. Analysis of the December 2004 tsunami that hit 13 countries and killed more than 300,000 people shows that areas in which strict environmental regulations led to the protection of the mangroves fared far better than areas where mangrove forests had been removed.

> " Despite worldwide attention to the plight of the Amazon rain forest, the deforestation rate appears to be increasing. "

The Amazon Rain Forest

Many of the concerns today center around the rain forests of the Amazon River basin of South America. The Amazon rain forest is a vast tract of land that covers more than 1 billion acres (405 million ha). Sixty percent of the rain forest is located in Brazil. Peru has roughly 13 percent of the rain forest; there is also acreage in Colombia, Venezuela, Ecuador, Bolivia, Guyana, Suriname, and French Guiana. About 140 indigenous tribes call the rain forest home.

Much of the attention to the Amazon rain forest is due to its rich natural resources. The Amazon comprises the largest and most species-rich tract of tropical rain forest in the world. In his 1984 book, world-renowned biologist Norman Myers called the area the "single richest region of the tropical biome"[14]—a description that scientists have continued to use. Some experts estimate that 0.4 square miles (1 square km) may contain over 75,000 types of trees and 150,000 plant species.

Most of the deforestation of the Amazon rain forest has occurred since the 1970s, when Brazil changed its land-use policies. "In the 1970s, Brazil's military dictatorship pursued a policy of 'integrar para não entregar,' meaning 'occupy it or risk losing it,'" explains a *National Geographic* article.[15] Poverty-stricken Brazilians moved into the jungle, clearing it for agriculture and carving a living out of the harsh environment. When the soils proved too poor to farm, they slashed and burned new areas, adding to the deforestation of greater and greater areas. Today much of the cleared land, with soils too poor for farming, is used for cattle ranching.

Despite worldwide attention to the plight of the Amazon rain forest, the deforestation rate appears to be increasing. According to FAO statistics, 163,436 square miles (423,297 sq. km) in Brazil's Amazon was deforested between 1990 and 2005; Mongabay.com, a rain forest conservation Web site, says that FAO estimates are lower than actual figures.

> " Although many of the world's poorest areas are most at risk of deforestation, industrialized nations are not immune to the problem. "

Some people say that focusing on the amount of land that has been lost distorts the issue. "When the World Wide Fund for Nature told us . . . [that] the Amazon rainforest loss is increasing to 1,489,600 hectares a year, we also have to ask, how much is that? Is it a lot?" writes the author of *The Skeptical Environmentalist*. "Perhaps a more important piece of information is that the total forest loss in the Amazon since the arrival of man has only amounted to 14 percent."[16]

Still, environmentalists warn that the Amazon will continue to lose forests as long as there are people living there. In 2005, 54 percent of the Brazilian Amazon was under some type of human pressure—up from 47 percent in 2002. According to the National Institute for Space Research, from August 2007 to August 2008, some 3,088 square miles (8,000 sq. km) of forest were destroyed—a 69 percent increase over the previous 12 months (1,861 square miles, or 4,820 sq. km). Although this increase came after three steady years of declining rates, experts fear that change may come too late. In a December 2007 report, the WWF warned that almost 60 percent of the Amazon rain forest could be destroyed by 2030. "The 'point of no return,' in which extensive degradation of the rainforest occurs and conservation prospects are greatly reduced, is just 15–25 years away—much sooner than some models suggest," the report concludes.[17]

Indonesia

Indonesia, a chain of islands in the South Pacific, has one of the highest rates of deforestation in the world. On average, about 2.5 million acres (1 million ha) of forest were cleared per year in the 1980s; today the average is 4.7 million acres (1.9 million ha) per year. Indonesia has cleared 40 percent of the forests that existed in 1950, including almost all of the forests on the islands of Sulawesi and Sumatra. Over half of the forests that remain are fragmented by logging roads or other access routes. Most at risk are Indonesia's lowland tropical forests, which are rich in timber resources.

> **Although experts disagree about the extent of deforestation, most agree that the loss of forests could have a long-term impact on the health of the Earth and its inhabitants.**

Much of the loss of Indonesia's forests is due to large-scale logging of timber, which began in the 1970s. Logging accelerated in recent years as Indonesia took over the role of supplying wood to nations such as Japan after the Philippines forests were exhausted. Indonesia's forests are also being cleared for small-scale farming and for commercial plantations of palm oil trees, which provide the world with much of its cooking oils. Illegal logging is of particular concern in Indonesia: Indonesia's government estimates that more than 25 million acres (10 million ha) of its forests have been cut illegally.

In October 2008 Greenpeace warned that if Indonesia does not eliminate rapid deforestation in the country, its forests could be gone in 10 years. "The forests of Papua are under heavy pressure from palm oil expansion, logging operations and other drivers of forest destruction," says Bustar Maitar, a forest campaigner with Greenpeace Southeast Asia. "We all need to play our part in safeguarding Indonesia's forests and the global climate by calling on the Indonesian Government to declare a moratorium on deforestation now."[18]

Africa

Africa, which has about 16 percent of the world's forests, is losing its forests at a higher rate than any other continent. The FAO indicates that the continent lost more than 9 percent of its forest area from 1990 to 2005, but some experts suggest that the rate of deforestation in Africa may actually be much higher. Some African countries have little or no forest remaining.

Statistics suggest that the rain forests that were once abundant in west and central Africa are almost depleted in many countries. One recent study showed that 90 percent of West Africa's coastal rain forests have disappeared since 1900. In an article titled "Goodbye to West Africa's Rainforests," Rhett A. Butler writes that the area's "once verdant and extensive rainforests are now a historical footnote. Gone to build ships and furniture, feed hungry mouths, and supply minerals and gems to the West, the band of tropical forests that once extended from Guinea to Cameroon are virtually gone."[19]

Deforestation rates are particularly high in Nigeria. Between 2000 and 2005, that country lost 55.7 percent of its primary forests. Logging, subsistence agriculture in which people rely on farming for their daily needs, and the collection of fuel wood are cited as leading causes of deforestation in Nigeria. Madagascar, too, has high rates of deforestation. The island of Comoros, north of Madagascar, has cleared almost 60 percent of its forests since 1990, and Burundi, a small country in central Africa, has cleared 47 percent.

North America and Europe

Although many of the world's poorest areas are most at risk of deforestation, industrialized nations are not immune to the problem. Many industrialized countries have already cut down most of their forests, and others continue to do so. In parts of the United States, Canada, and Australia, forests continue to be cleared to make way for development or commercial agriculture. Problems resulting from industrialization, such as acid rain, also contribute to the loss of forests in parts of Europe.

Until recently, the boreal forests of northern Scandinavia and Russia remained relatively untouched, but they, too, are undergoing change. Environmentalists stress that the lower levels of deforestation rates in many of these areas do not tell the whole story. Scandinavian countries have sound management practices in which foresters replace trees, usually several for each tree cut down. The replacements typically consist of a single tree species, however. These forests cannot support the same amount of wildlife. The lack of biodiversity also may put the forests at greater risk of degradation and deforestation.

Into the Future

Although experts disagree about the extent of deforestation, most agree that the loss of forests could have a long-term impact on the health of the Earth and its inhabitants. Many of the countries in which deforestation is a problem are those with the greatest amount of primary forestland. As one country becomes depleted of its valuable forests, another steps in to meet the world market for wood and other forest products. Deforestation is of particular concern in countries with high levels of poverty, many of which are home to the world's most ecologically valuable forests.

How Serious Is Deforestation?

66 It doesn't matter what agent causes disturbance to the forest, as soon as the disturbance is stopped . . . the forest immediately begins a process of recovery and will always recover—eventually. 99

—Patrick Moore, "Green Guru Sees the Good for the Tree," *Age*, December 16, 2006.

Moore is an outspoken advocate of sustainable forestry and the chair and chief scientist of Greenspirit, a consultancy focusing on environmental policy and communications in natural resources, biodiversity, energy, and climate change.

66 Even where forests have recovered, there is the likelihood that they have passed through an ecological point of no return. Perhaps someday . . . tropical forests will come back. But there will be no bringing back all the creatures who lived among them. 99

—Editorial, "Reforestation and Deforestation," *New York Times*, November 20, 2006.

The *New York Times* editorial board writes opinion pieces for that newspaper.

Bracketed quotes indicate conflicting positions.

* Editor's Note: While the definition of a primary source can be narrowly or broadly defined, for the purposes of Compact Research, a primary source consists of: 1) results of original research presented by an organization or researcher; 2) eyewitness accounts of events, personal experience, or work experience; 3) first-person editorials offering pundits' opinions; 4) government officials presenting political plans and/or policies; 5) representatives of organizations presenting testimony or policy.

Primary Source Quotes

> 66 In the last 50 years—in the name of progress and profit—a single generation has wiped out over half of the world's irreplaceable forests. Every minute 50 acres of rainforest is destroyed. The rainforest people who have always lived in and protected the forest are being robbed of their homes, livelihoods, and even their lives. 99

—Sting, *The Rainforest Foundation Annual Review: 2006–2007*. www.rainforestfoundationuk.org.

Sting, a world-renowned rock singer, is the founding patron of the Rainforest Foundation.

> 66 Deforestation continues at an alarming level, particularly in many tropical countries. But at the same time there is an increasing trend of regeneration and plantations of forests around the world. 99

—Pekka Patosaari, Forest Leadership Conference, March 1, 2005.

Patosaari is the director of the United Nations Forum on Forests.

> 66 We see prospects for an end to deforestation; we do not make a forecast but it is possible. 99

—Pekka Kauppi, "Study Hopeful for World's Forests," US Journal Proceedings of the National Academy of Sciences, 2006.

Kauppi, a professor of environmental science and policy at the University of Helsinki, is an expert on global forest resources.

> 66 Current trends in agriculture and livestock expansion, fire, drought, and logging could clear or severely damage *55 per cent of the Amazon rainforest by the year 2030.* 99

—Daniel C. Nepstad, *The Amazon's Vicious Cycles*. Gland, Switzerland: WWF International, 2007.

Nepstad, a forest ecologist, is a senior scientist at Woods Hole Research Center in Falmouth, Massachusetts.

66 It is very important not to succumb to the fatalism that so often affects discussions of Amazonia. What happens depends on human decisions. **99**

—Philip Fearnside, quoted in Rhett A. Butler, "Amazon Conservation Efforts Must Come Soon to Save World's Largest Rainforest Says Leading Scientist," Mongabay.com, October 23, 2006. http://news.mongabay.com.

Fearnside, a research professor at the National Institute for Research in the Amazon in Manaus, Brazil, is recognized as one of the world's foremost experts on the Amazon rain forest.

66 Rain forest trees can live for centuries, even millennia, so none of us expected things to change too fast . . . but in just two decades—a wink of time for a thousand-year-old tree—the ecosystem has been seriously degraded. **99**

—William Laurance, quoted in Jerome Douglas, "Amazon Rainforest Destruction Accelerated by Fragmentation," NaturalNews.com, November 29, 2006. www.naturalnews.com.

Laurance, a conservation biologist, is a staff scientist at the Smithsonian Tropical Research Institute and an expert on the deforestation of the Amazon.

66 Trends such as slowing population growth and intense urbanization give reason to hope that deforestation will slow, regeneration will accelerate, and mass extinction of tropical forest species will be avoided. **99**

—S. Joseph Wright and Helene C. Muller-Landau, "The Future of Tropical Forest Species," *Biotropica*, March 28, 2006.

Wright is a program director at the Smithsonian Tropical Research Institute and a leading authority on tropical plant biology. Mueller-Landau is an assistant professor in the Department of Ecology, Evolution, and Behavior at the University of Minnesota.

Facts and Illustrations

How Serious Is Deforestation?

- The world has **9.9 billion acres** (4 billion ha) of forest, covering about **30 percent** of the world's land area.

- Five countries—Russia, Brazil, Canada, the United States, and China —together account for more than half the world's forest area. Russia has more than **20 percent** of the world's forests.

- Globally, **36 percent** of forests are categorized as primary forests (forests of native species in which there are no clearly visible indications of human activity and ecological processes are not significantly disturbed). **Seventy-five percent** of the forested area in Latin America and the Caribbean is classified as primary forest; **45 percent** in North America.

- According to the World Resources Institute, more than **80 percent** of the Earth's natural forests already have been destroyed.

- The world loses almost **50,000 acres** (20,000 ha) of forestland a day.

- From 1990 to 2005, the world lost **3 percent** of its total forest area.

- From 2000 to 2005, **57 countries reported a rise** in their forest area, and **83 reported a drop**. Thirty-six of the countries reporting a decrease in forest area had a rate of higher than 1 percent per year.

Forests Past and Present

Over 6 billion hectares of forests blanketed the Earth 8,000 years ago; less than 4 billion hectares of forest remains today. Much of what remains is degraded and fragmented. Environmentalists are particularly concerned about preserving tropical forests, which are home to rich biodiversity.

Forest Distribution 8,000 Years Ago

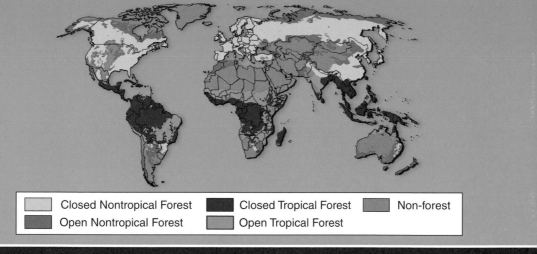

Closed Nontropical Forest	Closed Tropical Forest	Non-forest
Open Nontropical Forest	Open Tropical Forest	

Forest Distribution in 1990

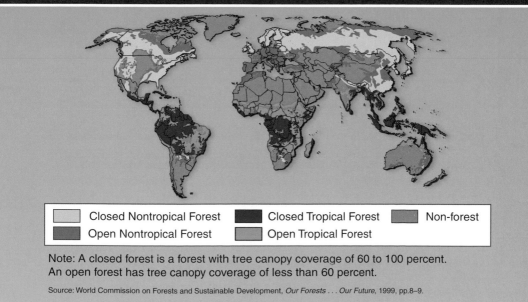

Closed Nontropical Forest	Closed Tropical Forest	Non-forest
Open Nontropical Forest	Open Tropical Forest	

Note: A closed forest is a forest with tree canopy coverage of 60 to 100 percent. An open forest has tree canopy coverage of less than 60 percent.

Source: World Commission on Forests and Sustainable Development, *Our Forests . . . Our Future*, 1999, pp.8–9.

Deforestation

Forests Are Unequally Distributed

Based on 2005 data, this chart shows the 10 countries that have the largest forest area. These 10 countries have 66 percent of the world's forest area. These countries play a particularly important role in the future of the world's forests. If countries with substantial forests fail to enact and enforce laws to protect the forests within their borders, the remaining intact, old-growth forests will be at risk of deforestation.

Numbers in million hectares

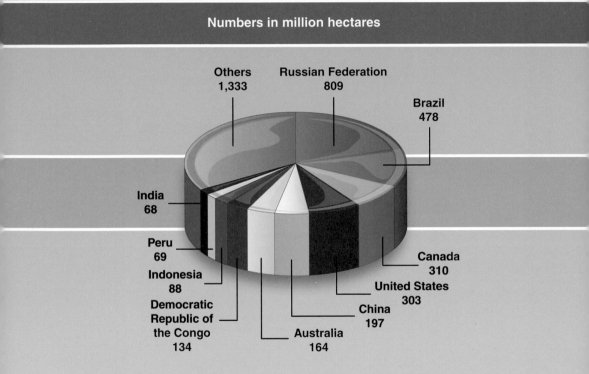

Others 1,333
Russian Federation 809
Brazil 478
India 68
Peru 69
Indonesia 88
Democratic Republic of the Congo 134
Australia 164
China 197
United States 303
Canada 310

Source: Food and Agriculture Organization, *Global Forest Resources Assessment 2005: 15 Key Findings*, Rome: FAO, 2006.

- The highest rates of deforestation are in **Africa, Latin America, and the Caribbean**.

- Brazil has **30 percent** of the total amount of rain forest in the world. In 2002 about **47 percent** of the Brazilian Amazon was under some type of human pressure. Recent estimates comparing this figure with new data from 2005 show that human pressure has increased by **7 percent**.

Percentage of Forest Lost Since 1990

This chart shows the 20 countries that cleared the greatest percentage of their remaining forest cover between 1990 and 2005. As shown, African countries are at particular risk of stripping their land of forest cover. Comoros, a small island nation north of Madagascar, cleared over 50 percent of its forests in just 15 years. Experts disagree about the direct cause of the deforestation, but poverty is a major underlying issue that contributes to the loss of forests in most of these countries.

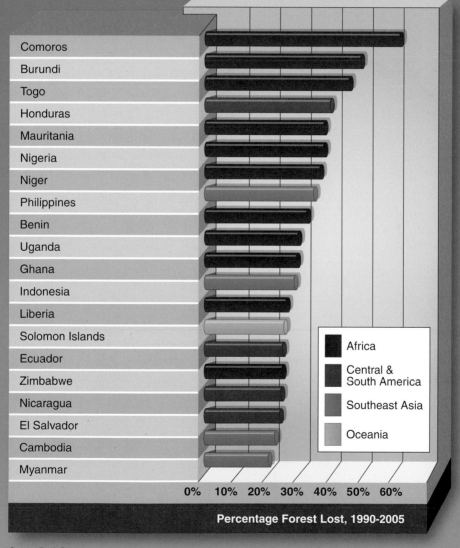

Comoros
Burundi
Togo
Honduras
Mauritania
Nigeria
Niger
Philippines
Benin
Uganda
Ghana
Indonesia
Liberia
Solomon Islands
Ecuador
Zimbabwe
Nicaragua
El Salvador
Cambodia
Myanmar

0% 10% 20% 30% 40% 50% 60%

Percentage Forest Lost, 1990-2005

Africa
Central & South America
Southeast Asia
Oceania

Source: *Earth Observatory*, NASA, "Tropical Deforestation," March 30, 2007. Data from the Food and Agriculture Organization of the United Nations' Global Forest Resources Assessment Report 2005.

What Causes Deforestation?

66God has cared for these trees, saved them from drought, disease, avalanches, and a thousand tempests and floods. But he cannot save them from fools.99

—John Muir, renowned naturalist and author.

66Deforestation in tropical countries is often driven by the perverse economic reality that forests are worth more dead than alive.99

—Center for International Forestry Research, Indonesia.

Although people disagree about the extent of the various factors that contribute to deforestation, there is general consensus that the most serious direct causes include the conversion of the land for agriculture and ranching. Also to blame are unsustainable logging practices and forest fires—often set intentionally to clear the land. In some places, mining and oil and gas exploration also have a major impact.

In addition, there are several factors that have a more indirect impact on forests. Most experts believe poverty to be a major contributor to deforestation. Poor people often clear forestland to plant crops or for the other resources found there. The land management policies of some countries have escalated deforestation by encouraging poor people to settle in forested areas. Economic policies involving subsidies and taxes may also contribute to the problem.

The common way to clear forested land for agriculture or ranching is by felling and burning trees. Slash-and-burn techniques have been used for centuries by people who have come to be known as "shifting cultivators"—that is, people who grow crops and move on when the soil is depleted. Today, however, roughly 300 million people worldwide depend on slash-and-burn agriculture—10 times as many people as a century ago. As a result, people are moving deeper into the forests and trying to plant crops on less fertile soils. Norman Myers, a renowned biologist, says that slash-and-burn agriculture is responsible for more than half of the loss of forests today.

Slash-and-burn techniques can be particularly devastating for rain forests. Rain forest soils are low in nutrients, so it takes just a few years before they are unable to support crops. When farming is no longer viable, the land often is used for grazing. In some places, farmers plant rice or other crops for just a year before turning it over to cattle grazing. "This is a death sentence for the soil, as cattle remove the last scarce traces of fertility," says the World Rainforest Movement. "The result is an entirely degraded piece of land which will be unable to recover its original biomass for many years."[20]

Industrial Agriculture

As subsistence farming gives way to industrial agriculture, there is often additional risk to forests. In Thailand, for instance, huge areas of tropical rain forest have been cleared to grow cassava, which is turned into tapioca and used in Europe to feed pigs. From 1965 to 1995, the land used for cassava cultivation grew from 250,000 acres to over 2,500,000 acres (100,000 ha to over 1 million ha).

In Malaysia and Indonesia, vast tracts of tropical forest have been cleared to make way for commercial palm tree plantations to meet the growing demand for vegetable oil and biofuels. Globally, the palm oil area increased by 43 percent in just a decade, and the Indonesian government has given permits to palm oil corporations for an additional 10 million acres (4 million ha), much of which is forested land.

> **Most experts believe poverty to be a major contributor to deforestation.**

Deforestation can also be traced to soybean cultivation. Soy provides more than one-fourth of the world's vegetable oil. South American countries are meeting much of this global demand; soy is the biggest agricultural export of Brazil and Bolivia. In 2004 soy accounted for over 25 percent of Bolivia's total export revenues. Between 1961 and 2002, the area under soybean production in Brazil increased by 57 times. Experts predict that growing demand for biofuels could cause additional land to be cleared for soybeans.

Cattle Ranching

Cattle ranching is a major source of deforestation in Latin America. During the 1970s and 1980s, stretches of rain forest were burned and converted into cattle pastures. "In a few short years, overgrazing, compaction [the compression of the soil] and nutrient loss turn cleared forest lands into eroded wastelands,"[21] writes the FAO.

> In Malaysia and Indonesia, vast tracts of tropical forest have been cleared to make way for commercial palm tree plantations to meet the growing demand for vegetable oil and biofuels.

In the 1970s and 1980s, U.S. companies purchased large tracts of forest in Costa Rica to raise cattle to meet fast-food restaurants' growing demand for cheap beef, contributing to the high rate of deforestation in that country. In 2004, 300 million pounds (136 million kg) of beef were exported from Central America to the United States. Today cattle ranching has moved southward to the Amazon. Between 1990 and 2002, the number of cattle in Brazil more than doubled; 80 percent of this growth took place in the Amazon.

Wood and Wood Products

The forest products industry is a large part of the economy in both developed and developing countries. People throughout the world depend on wood for shelter and fuel. In fact, almost 3 billion people in developing countries rely on wood for heating and cooking. For example, wood and charcoal, which is produced by heating wood, are the preferred cooking and heating fuels in Malawi; the World Bank estimated in 2001 that charcoal consumption alone was twice what Malawi's woodlands could sustain without further deforestation. Loggers there illegally clear 100 square miles (259 sq. km) of forest each year just to meet the demand for charcoal.

Billions more people use wood to build homes and furniture. Trees are also cut down to make packaging, paper, and many other products. Logging provides the raw goods for these products. Much of this logging is carried on illegally. Today logging may be the greatest threat to forests in central Africa, eastern Siberia, British Columbia, and the Guianas.

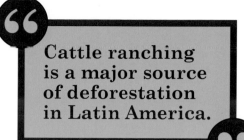

Cattle ranching is a major source of deforestation in Latin America.

Commercial Logging

Some of the logging is carried out by large, international corporations. Industry experts say that these companies have an investment in the future of their land, so they use practices that protect the forest. Some use selective logging—a practice in which only some of the mature trees are selected for cutting. When done correctly, selective logging ensures that a forest regrows naturally.

Selective logging does not always protect the forest, however. Experts warn that harvesting just one or two valuable species can take a heavy toll. Moreover, because the forest canopy may remain with selective logging, it is not always easy to tell the extent of deforestation or degradation. Thinning out the forests also leaves them drier and more susceptible to fire. The haze that blanketed Southeast Asia in 1997 was in fact the result of extensive fires burning unchecked through drought-stricken forests. In Indonesia alone, an area at least the size of New Jersey was burned.

Clear-Cutting

Many people argue that it is not logging itself that causes deforestation, but the practice of clearing entire fields of all their trees, a practice called clear-cutting. In the early 1990s, Canada and Malaysia were among the countries in which logging companies ruthlessly cleared thousands of miles of primary forests. In Vancouver Island, Canada, where forestry accounts for half the island's income, entire mountains have been stripped of the forests that thrived there for centuries.

Forestry is big business. In countries large and small, powerful multinational corporations are involved in harvesting and selling valuable hardwoods by clear-cutting the forests. The extraction and consumption of tropical hardwoods has been so massive that some countries that once led the export market have exhausted their supplies. The demand for hardwoods for construction, furniture, and other uses has contributed to deforestation in the Philippines, Malaysia, the Ivory Coast, Nigeria, and Thailand. Of particular concern to environmentalists is the growing demand for rare, exotic hardwoods that are only found in intact tropical forests. The demand for precious tropical hardwoods has multiplied nearly 25 times over the last 40 years. Currently, 99 percent of tropical hardwoods sold are taken from old-growth tropical rain forests.

> " The demand for hardwoods . . . has contributed to deforestation in the Philippines, Malaysia, the Ivory Coast, Nigeria, and Thailand. "

Clear-cutting is used not only to harvest the trees that are in a forest. A forest may also be clear-cut to make room for housing or industry, the trees burned or otherwise disposed of. In Indonesia, thousands of acres of forests have been cleared to make room for palm oil plantations.

Most environmentalists oppose logging operations, but Patrick Moore, who cofounded Greenpeace in 1971, thinks the environmental movement overestimates the damage that results from cutting down trees. Throughout history forests have replenished themselves naturally. Moore writes, "It is an ecological fact that many types of forest ecosystems function most successfully when they are periodically cleared and allowed to regrow anew from the clearing."[22]

Mining and Oil and Gas Extraction

Precious metals and gems are found in forests around the world. But extracting these natural resources is a destructive activity that can damage the forest ecosystem and contribute to deforestation. Large-scale mining operations often clear large tracts of land for open pits. Illegal mining is a particular problem. Wildcat miners enter along the roads that mining companies have built and use explosives to clear entire hillsides in search of riches.

Some deforestation has also occurred as oil and gas companies have opened up forested areas. Texaco entered *El Oriente*, a region of the Amazon in Ecuador, in 1967, bringing with it a lucrative export. "Over time it became obvious that this windfall was a poor blessing," writes the WWF; "the substantial oil revenues and royalties were used by the government to build roads and subsidize cattle ranching and agriculture, causing large-scale deforestation."[23] Similarly, the opening of a huge gas field in Peru's Amazonian region has altered drainage patterns and interrupted the natural forest ecosystem there.

Commercial logging, mining, and oil and gas extraction require roads. Although the roads themselves may require a limited amount of clearing, they provide access to forested areas. In many places, people follow the roads into the interior forest and cut down trees for wood or clear areas along the road for farming. Studies suggest that roads also leave the forest more susceptible to fire because they increase the dryness of the remaining trees and contribute to other negative edge effects.

> In many areas of the world, large numbers of poor people are being pushed out of crowded cities into rural areas, where the forests are cleared for fuelwood or to make room for farming.

Population Growth

Experts disagree about the impact of population growth on deforestation. The Population Reference Bureau reports, "An overview of studies conducted in the 1980s and 1990s reveals a strong relationship between population growth and deforestation in Central America, East and West Africa, and South Asia, but a much less clear association in Amazonia (South America) and Central Africa."[24] Rhett A. Butler elaborates further: "The ultimate driving force behind all deforestation is human overpopulation; both the population in the temperate region that places demands on the resources derived from the tropical rainforests, and the expanding population of developing tropical nations, who exploit the rainforest for survival."[25]

Still, it appears that it depends more on the nature of the population increase than on the numbers themselves. Where poor people rely on the forest for subsistence, population increases likely contribute to deforestation. Where people rely less directly on the land for food, forests are less threatened. Most of the forests in the eastern United States, for instance, were gone by 1920, but they have experienced regrowth as people have moved from isolated farms to urban centers. Still, in many places, as cities grow larger to accommodate more people, trees are cut down to make more room for houses and roads. National policies also make a difference. In India, forest area increased in the 1990s (mostly through tree plantation programs) even as the country experienced double-digit population growth.

> The demand for forest products in one region of the world can fuel deforestation in another.

Poverty

Most experts believe that poverty is an underlying cause of deforestation. Haiti has just 1 percent of its original forest cover. Much of the deforestation of this country, experts say, has resulted from the population's desperate search for fuelwood. In contrast, neighboring Dominican Republic, which has a far stronger economy, still has much of its primary forest intact.

In many areas of the world, large numbers of poor people are being pushed out of crowded cities into rural areas, where the forests are cleared for fuelwood or to make room for farming. Over the past 10 years, an estimated 1 million Indonesian families have moved from the overcrowded island of Sumatra to outlying islands, where they have cut down rain forests to grow rice and other crops. Experts believe that government policies in Mexico and Brazil that encouraged poor people to take up farming contributed to increasing deforestation in those countries.

Just because people are poor does not mean they will turn to the forests. Too often, national policies or laws play a key role in encouraging deforestation. Some countries support the timber industry; others have policies that encourage—or at least condone—poor forestry practices. Some countries also offer subsidies for wood processing or plantation programs that encourage the conversion of forestland to other uses. Policies that grant title only to cleared land and programs that encourage people to move from overpopulated urban areas also are contributing factors, particularly in poor countries. For instance, the Brazilian government in the past has offered free land to people willing to move to the Amazon basin and has subsidized cattle ranching there. In addition, some countries have tax structures that discourage investment in forest planting or conservation.

Ecuador is just one example of where land use policies have encouraged deforestation. Since the 1970s there has been a great influx of farmers into the Ecuadorian Amazon, one of the most precious forest areas in the world. Most of these farmers came from the Andes and coastal regions of the country, where they experienced landlessness, unemployment, and land degradation. Migration was strongly encouraged by the Ecuadorian government, which gave migrants land titles for "useful" land. Untouched forestland was not considered "useful," so it would not be eligible for such titles; people could obtain ownership only if they worked the land. The conversion of forests into farms was the logical result.

World View

Deforestation is a global problem. The demand for forest products in one region of the world can fuel deforestation in another. Debtor nations may be particularly tempted to sell off forest assets to reduce the amount they owe. International aid can also inadvertently add to the problem. Many tropical countries have borrowed money from the World Bank and other institutions for development projects. To repay these debts, these countries are under pressure to cut down their forests to sell the timber or for plantation agriculture. In addition, infrastructure programs, such as the construction of hydroelectric dams or highways, may expose virgin forestlands to new stresses.

Primary Source Quotes*

What Causes Deforestation?

66 **Fast food giants like McDonald's are trashing the Amazon for cheap meat. Every time you buy a Chicken McNugget you could be taking a bite out of the Amazon.**99

—Gavin Edwards, "Greenpeace Investigation Links Fast Food Giants to Amazon Destruction," press release, Greenpeace, April 6, 2006.

Edwards is the forests campaign coordinator at Greenpeace International.

66 **Is there a relationship between beef production, U.S. beef consumption and rainforest deforestation to raise beef cattle? Simply put—No.**99

—Beef Myths, "Beef Production—Rainforest Deforestation to Raise Beef," 2007. www.beefmyths.org.

Beef Myths is a Web site intended to counter the negative stereotypes of the beef industry.

Bracketed quotes indicate conflicting positions.

* Editor's Note: While the definition of a primary source can be narrowly or broadly defined, for the purposes of Compact Research, a primary source consists of: 1) results of original research presented by an organization or researcher; 2) eyewitness accounts of events, personal experience, or work experience; 3) first-person editorials offering pundits' opinions; 4) government officials presenting political plans and/or policies; 5) representatives of organizations presenting testimony or policy.

66 **Deforestation is nearly always caused by friendly farmers growing our food, and by nice carpenters building our houses, towns, and cities. Deforestation is not an evil plot, it is something we do on purpose in order to feed and house the 6 billion and growing human population.** 99

—Patrick Moore, "Trees Are the Answer," Greenspirit, www.greenspirit.com.

Moore is an outspoken advocate of sustainable forestry and the chairman and chief scientist of Greenspirit, a consultancy focusing on environmental policy and communications in natural resources, biodiversity, energy, and climate.

66 **Deforestation will continue as long as cutting down and burning trees is more economic than preserving them.** 99

—Johan Eliasch, "Eliasch Review on International Deforestation Published," press release, International Forest, October 14, 2008.

Eliasch, the United Kingdom's Special Representative on Deforestation, was commissioned by England's prime minister to report on deforestation.

66 **Regardless of the international and national policies in place, deforestation cannot be combated effectively unless local landowners and residents have more reason to protect forest ecosystems than they have to destroy them.** 99

—Avoided Deforestation Partners, "Why Communities?" press release, Avoided Deforestation Partners.org, May 27, 2007.

Avoided Deforestation Partners is an international network of leaders in carbon policy, finance, forestry, and conservation founded in May 2007 to support international efforts to halt tropical deforestation.

66 **We have no money to raise our families. We have nowhere to run, nothing else to do. So we have to cut the trees to feed our families.** 99

—Injes Juma, quoted in Michael Wines, "Malawi Is Burning, and Deforestation Erodes Economy," *New York Times*, November 1, 2005.

Juma is among the many of the world's impoverished people who illegally cut and sell firewood and charcoal at roadside stands to support their families.

> **❝Logging is a key, if indirect, driver of Amazonian forest destruction.❞**

—William Laurance, "Amazon Rain Forest Not Helped by 'Light' Logging," *National Geographic News*, April 1, 2006. http://news.nationalgeographic.com.

Laurance, a conservation biologist, is a staff scientist at the Smithsonian Tropical Research Institute and an expert on the deforestation of the Amazon.

> **❝Logging rarely leads directly to deforestation in the Amazon. Most loggers only remove a small number of trees per hectare.❞**

—David Kaimowitz et al., "Hamburger Connection Fuels Amazon Destruction," Center for International Forestry Research, April 2004.

The Center for International Forestry Research is an international organization that conducts research to inform policies and practices that affect forests in developing countries.

> **❝One of the greatest threats to the world's environment is the compounding numbers of rural poor who turn increasingly to the rainforests to feed and shelter themselves.❞**

—Rhett A. Butler, "Population and Poverty," Mongabay.com, August 2007.

Butler has been working on rain forest issues since 1995 and manages the Web site Mongabay.com, which aims to raise interest in wildlife and wildlands and to promote awareness of environmental issues.

> **❝It is said that people destroy forests because they are poor, and that deforestation causes poverty—but generalizations are a poor foundation for policy. We find that deforestation is caused by both rich and poor people—and it can either destroy or create assets for poor people.❞**

—Kenneth M. Chomitz, "World Bank Advises Better Forest Governance and Use of Carbon Markets to Save Tropical Forests," press release, World Bank, October 23, 2006.

Chomitz is the lead author of *At Loggerheads? Agricultural Expansion, Poverty Reduction, and Environment in the Tropical Forests*, a 2007 World Bank report exploring the relationship between deforestation, agriculture, and poverty.

What Causes Deforestation?

- The FAO estimates that **90 percent** of deforestation is caused by unsustainable agricultural practices.

- Less than **10 percent** of Amazonian soils are suitable for sustained conventional agriculture. Most land in the area is exhausted within 3 or 4 years.

- There are **20.7 million acres** (8.4 million ha) of cattle ranches in Brazil, averaging 59,300 acres (24,000ha) in size.

- According to Rainforest Action Network, **300 million pounds** (136 million kg) of beef are imported to the United States from Central America alone.

- According to the FAO, the production of wood and nonwood resources is the primary use for **34 percent** of the world's forests.

- **Sixty percent** of wood harvested worldwide is used for energy, mainly for cooking and heating in developing countries; **25 percent** is for construction of buildings and furniture; and **15 percent** is used to manufacture pulp and paper.

- Over **90 percent** of the wood harvested in Africa is used locally for fuel.

The Main Causes of Tropical Deforestation

The reasons for deforestation vary, depending on the region, and even the country. Agriculture is the main cause of tropical deforestation. Particularly damaging is the slash-and-burn agriculture practiced by small-scale farmers. Commercial agriculture—particularly palm oil plantations and soybean cultivation—also play a role. In some places, commercial farmers may not clear much forest directly, but they push ranchers and slash-and-burn farmers deeper into the forest, resulting in the clearing of virgin forests. Cattle ranching and logging also are main causes of deforestation in many areas.

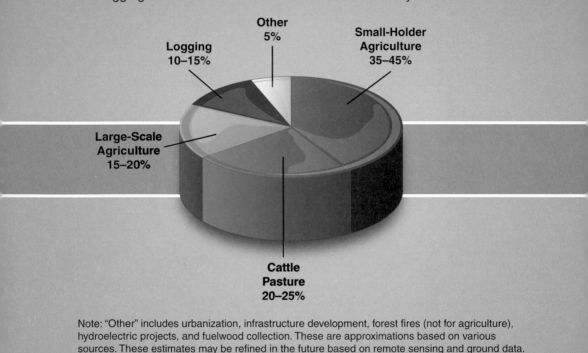

Other
5%

Small-Holder
Agriculture
35–45%

Logging
10–15%

Large-Scale
Agriculture
15–20%

Cattle
Pasture
20–25%

Note: "Other" includes urbanization, infrastructure development, forest fires (not for agriculture), hydroelectric projects, and fuelwood collection. These are approximations based on various sources. These estimates may be refined in the future based on remote sensing and ground data.

Source: Rhett A. Butler, "Causes of Tropical Deforestation: 2000–2005." www.mongabay.com.

- Roughly **20,000 square miles** (51,800 sq. km) of tropical forest is logged annually. Loggers take only between 4 and 10 percent of the trees but leave much of the land surface bare and open to erosion.

- About **80 percent** of the total area deforested in the Amazon is located within 20 miles (30 km) of official roads.

Cattle Ranching and Deforestation in Central America

Cattle ranching has contributed greatly to the deforestation of Central America's forests over the past 40 years, in part fueled by the U.S. demand for cheap beef. Although cattle sometimes graze on land that was initially cleared for agriculture, this line graph shows the relationship between pastureland and the loss of forests. As more land is cleared for cattle and pastures the forest area decreases.

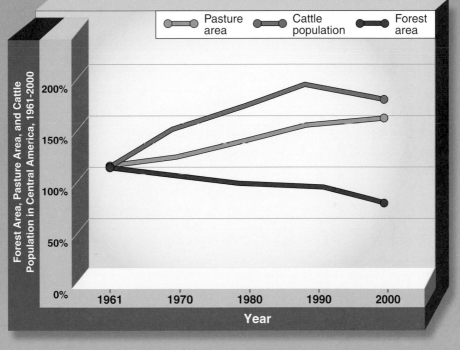

Source: Food and Agriculture Organization, 2006. "Cattle Ranching and Deforestation," Livestock Policy Brief 03, p. 2.

- An estimated **300 million** people worldwide depend on slash-and-burn agriculture, a main cause of deforestation.

- **Six times** as much of the land cleared in the Amazon is used for pasture than for crops.

Roads Contribute to Deforestation

Much of the deforested land in the Amazon rain forest is near roads. If current trends in agriculture expansion are extended into the future, with the most likely road-paving projects completed over the next 2 decades, by 2050 over 800,000 square miles (2 million sq. km)—an area the size of Mexico—will be deforested. Experts believe that roads are one of the main causes of deforestation because people follow the roads into the interior of the forest, clearing and settling on the land. In some countries, access results in poaching, illegal logging, slash-and-burn agriculture, and other harmful uses of forestland. Roads also fragment the forest and contribute to the edge effect, increasing the risk of forest fires and flooding.

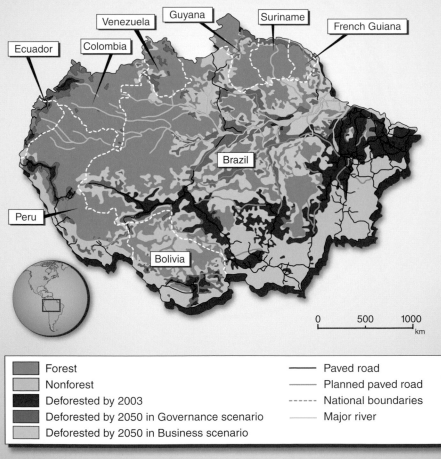

Source: Giulio Volpi, "Climate Mitigation, Deforestation and Human Development in Brazil," Human Development Paper 2007/2008, New York: United Nations Development Programme, 2008, p. 22.

Palm Oil and Deforestation in Asia

Together, Malaysia and Indonesia make up about 87 percent of the world's total palm oil production. In 2007, Indonesia surpassed Malaysia to become the world leader in palm oil production and is forecast to increase its production by about 10 percent a year. Environmentalists say that vast tracts of forest are being cleared in Indonesia to make way for the palm oil plantations. Increasing demand for biofuels is one of the main reasons for the increase.

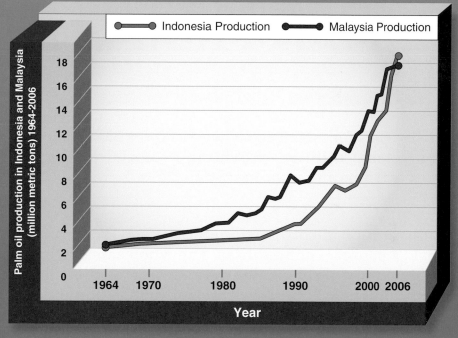

Source: Rhett A. Butler, "U.S. Biofuels Policy Drives Deforestation in Indonesia, the Amazon," mongabay.com, January 17, 2008. http://news.mongabay.com.

- Worldwide demand for fuelwood and charcoal is growing steadily at about **1.1 percent** per year.

- The demand for tropical hardwoods is **25 times higher** today than 40 years ago. Currently, **99 percent** of this demand is met from hardwoods taken from old-growth rain forests.

What Are the Consequences of Deforestation?

66 The world's forests need to be seen for what they are—giant global utilities, providing essential public services to humanity on a vast scale. 99

—Charles, Prince of Wales.

66 Deforestation disproportionately affects some of the world's poorest communities. The wholesale cutting of tropical forests robs vulnerable people of their livelihoods and their identities, creating mobile populations that are prone to hunger, disease and conflict. 99

—Helene D. Gayle, president and CEO of CARE, an international nonprofit humanitarian organization.

The loss of forests has a number of environmental, economic, and social impacts, many of which are interrelated. The destruction of forests worldwide results in flooding, erosion, and landslides; contributes to the extinction of plants and animals and the loss of biodiversity; and drives human forest dwellers—such as the Karen of Burma, the Mapuche of Chile, and the Penan of Malaysia—from their homelands.

Floods

There are many examples of the devastating results of deforestation. Where forests have been removed, rainwater flows quickly over the surface of the land. Swiftly moving water also picks up sediment along the way, carrying it into rivers and streams, filling them with sand, silt, and soil and reducing their capacity to hold water. As water runs off the soil, it causes the overflow of rivers and floods the surrounding plains, sometimes within minutes.

Ongoing deforestation can have long-term impacts on the water system. In recent years the annual flood crest of the Amazon River has increased despite the fact that the rainfall levels have been lower than in the past. Scientists believe that this is due almost exclusively to deforestation and sediment flowing into the river.

> " Studies have shown that destruction of rain forests in Nigeria, Ghana, and other West African countries have contributed to severe droughts, causing widespread hunger and famine. "

Haiti, which is sometimes called the "desert of the Caribbean," is an example of how deforestation can put entire communities at risk. Over 98 percent of the forests on this once lush island have been cleared, mostly by impoverished Haitians who use wood and charcoal found there for cooking and heating. When Hurricane Jeanne hit in September 2004, hundreds of people on Haiti lost their lives to flash floods, compared with just 12 people in neighboring Dominican Republic, where there remain large tracts of forests.

Drought

Deforestation can contribute to desertification, a gradual process in which soils can no longer support life. Even where the landscape is not completely barren, the loss of forests can increase the number and severity of droughts. Tree roots funnel water into underground aquifers, where it is stored to supply rivers during dry spells. Studies have shown that destruction of rain forests in Nigeria, Ghana, and other West African countries have contributed to severe droughts, causing widespread hunger and famine. Forests once covered 35 percent of Ethiopia's land; today only 4 percent of that nation is forested. Scientists believe that the deforestation is a main contributor to the droughts and famines that routinely ravage the country.

Deforestation also decreases the amount of moisture evaporating into the atmosphere. Rather than being evaporated and then returning as rainfall, the water runs directly into oceans. According to one study, in deforested areas of China, the average annual precipitation decreased by one-third between the 1950s and the 1980s.

Soil Erosion and Landslides

In forests the nutrients are bound up in the vegetation, and the soils themselves are quite poor. When the trees are cut down, rain washes the essential nutrients from the soil into rivers and streams. Areas without trees also have fewer leaves, branches, and other tree litter to protect the soil from the scorching effect of the sun. As the soil temperature increases, nutrients such as nitrogen are lost, further reducing the fertility of the remaining soil.

As soil becomes depleted of nutrients, it is ruined for agriculture, causing more land to be needed for productive farming. Those who live in forest regions may be forced to move every year, clearing out new acreage to farm. A 2008 international conference on forest management concludes, "As the productivity and production of agricultural land declines, many communities with low adaptive capacity encroach into the forests for grazing, fuelwood, food and illicit harvesting for revenue generation, further enhancing their degradation."[26]

> Computer simulations of areas in which forests are converted to agricultural landscapes suggest that conditions in deforested areas are hotter and drier.

In hilly areas, soil erosion contributes to the risk of mudslides and landslides, putting lives and entire communities at risk. Deforestation is blamed for an increasing number of deadly landslides in Indonesia, for instance, where forests have been stripped to make way for palm oil plantations. In early 2008 landslides killed at least 107 people on Java, Indonesia's most populous island, and destroyed 1,600 homes. "These same issues can have more moderate effects closer to home," warns reporter Dan Shapley. "Many communities facing fast-paced suburban development have found that the clearing and paving of land causes severe drainage issues, leading to flooded roads and basements, degraded streams and the need for municipal investment in infrastructure, which drives up local taxes."[27]

Impact on Climate

The natural water cycle in forests also helps to mediate climate. Trees pump vast quantities of water from the ground. The water evaporates from their leaves, releasing moisture into the atmosphere, which then falls to the ground as rain. In tropical forests, roughly one-third of the rain is water that evaporates from tree leaves. Not only does this maintain a constant source of clean water, it also cools the Earth's surface. Computer simulations of areas in which forests are converted to agricultural landscapes suggest that conditions in deforested areas are hotter and drier.

Deforestation of boreal forests can also impact climate. A 2008 study found that boreal trees also release chemicals known as terpenes that help thicken the clouds above them, causing sunlight to be reflected back into space. Dominick Spracklen, one of the study's leaders, calls trees the planet's "air conditioners" and concludes that "cutting down trees could worsen climate change to a larger degree than was previously thought."[28]

Some scientists believe that deforestation can have implications worldwide. Deforestation is contributing to global warming, they say, as well as near-term changes in climate. Changes in the water cycle in one area can have an impact on weather patterns elsewhere. "Deforestation in the Amazon region of South America (Amazonia) influences rainfall from Mexico to Texas and in the Gulf of Mexico," says a NASA report. "Similarly, deforesting lands in Central Africa affects precipitation in the upper and lower U.S. Midwest, while deforestation in Southeast

> " Deforestation and unsustainable forest management practices increase water pollution, making local populations more vulnerable to disease. "

Asia was found to alter rainfall in China and the Balkan Peninsula."[29]

Not everyone agrees that climate change can be blamed on the loss of forests, however. "World weather is governed by the oceans—that great system of ocean atmospherics," writes Philip Stott. "Most things that happen on land are mere blips to the system, basically insignificant."[30]

Global Warming

As countries become increasingly concerned about global warming, many people are turning to forests for an answer. Trees store carbon dioxide—one of the greenhouse gases whose buildup in the atmosphere contributes to global warming. Some scientists estimate that the world's trees and soils contain 2 billion tons (1.8 billion metric tons) of carbon—85 percent of which is in forests. Former U.S. vice president Al Gore calls protecting the world's tropical forests "one of the most effective things we can do in the near term to address the climate crisis."[31]

> " As indigenous peoples vanish or are assimilated into the broader culture, their rich cultural history dies with them. "

Deforestation not only results in the loss of trees that store carbon, it also releases carbon into the atmosphere. Deforestation is thought to be responsible for about 20 percent of annual greenhouse gas emissions— more than all the world's cars, trucks, planes, and ships combined. In some developing countries, where forests are burned to make way for agriculture, more greenhouse gases come from deforestation than any other source.

Economic Impacts

At least 400 million people live in or near forests, including 60 million indigenous people who depend on forests almost entirely for their livelihood. Millions more make a living through subsistence agriculture, hunting and gathering, or low-impact harvesting of forest products such as rubber, nuts, or rattan. The people who depend directly on forests include the world's poorest residents. The World Bank says that 90 percent of the poorest of the poor—families living on less than a dollar a day—

depend substantially on forests for their livelihoods. For them, deforestation is devastating.

The forest is important to the inhabitants of wealthy countries as well. Worldwide, forest industries employ between 60 and 100 million people. As forests are depleted, there is increased risk of shortages of forest resources, particularly in developing countries that lack forest management policies and the means of enforcement.

Health

Deforestation and unsustainable forest management practices increase water pollution, making local populations more vulnerable to disease. More than 3 million deaths result from water pollution and poor sanitation annually, most of these in poor rural areas. Pekka Patosaari, the director of the United Nations Forum on Forests, laments, "Despite the close linkages between land use, forestry, fresh water and health, these sectors are rarely managed in a holistic manner."[32]

Health experts also raise concerns about the impact of deforestation on treatments for illness and disease. In many parts of the world, modern drugs are expensive and hard to find. In Africa, for instance, more than 80 percent of the population depends on medicinal plants for their medical needs. The loss of forests could make it difficult for poor people to get these medicines.

Forest resources also are important to human health in wealthier nations. Aspirin originally came from the bark of willow trees. Quinine, the treatment for malaria, comes from the bark of cinchona trees. Roughly 70 percent of the plants shown to have anticancer properties are found only in the rain forest.

> " While direct consequences may be obvious, it is difficult to assess the many indirect and long-term consequences that deforestation may have on the world and its inhabitants. "

Scientists suggest that we have only scratched the surface in exploring the medicinal properties of many plant species. Less than 1 percent of tropical plants have been involved in laboratory experiments to determine their potential as medicines. In a NASA article on tropical deforestation, the author writes, "Hidden in the genes of plants, animals, fungi, and bacteria that have not even been discovered yet may be cures for cancer and other diseases or the key to improving the yield and nutritional quality of foods—which the U.N. Food and Agriculture Organization says will be crucial for feeding the nearly ten billion people the Earth will likely need to support in coming decades."[33]

The Displacement of Indigenous Peoples

Forests have been inhabited by indigenous peoples for thousands of years, before the creation of most of today's nations. Deforestation—particularly when it results from the granting of land to large logging or mining companies—results in the displacement of many of these people and threatens their cultural history. Logging in Guyana has caused a flood of Kwebanna refugees to flee their ancestral homes and take refuge in Venezuela.

The fight over land can lead to violent confrontations. On February 12, 2005, a gunman shot and killed Dorothy Stang, an American-born nun and environmental activist, when she tried to stop them from illegally planting grass for livestock in a remote section of the Brazilian rain forest. Later that year, 3 children died when police used tear gas, riot sticks, and bulldozers to forcibly evict 450 people from a road blockade during a long-standing struggle of the U'wa against oil exploitation in a forest they claim as their ancestral territory. Survival International, an advocacy group for tribal peoples, says that after a large iron-ore mine was opened in the eastern Amazon, the indigenous Awa were pushed off the land that had been promised them and "shot, poisoned and tortured." Within 10 years, says the group, the Awa were "in danger of extinction."[34]

> **Anything that upsets the delicate balance of nature can have unforeseen repercussions.**

As indigenous peoples vanish or are assimilated into the broader culture, their rich cultural history dies with them. Rhett A. Butler, who has worked for many years on behalf of tropical rain forests, warns that we may be losing invaluable information about medicinal cures:

No one understands the secrets of [medicinal] plants better than indigenous shamans—medicine men and women—who have developed boundless knowledge of this library of flora for curing everything from foot rot to diabetes. But like the forests themselves, the knowledge of these botanical wizards is fast-disappearing due to deforestation and profound cultural transformation among younger generations. The combined loss of this knowledge and these forests irreplaceably impoverishes the world of cultural and biological diversity.[35]

The Future

While direct consequences may be obvious, it is difficult to assess the many indirect and long-term consequences that deforestation may have on the world and its inhabitants. Anything that upsets the delicate balance of nature can have unforeseen repercussions. Some consequences we may only learn of when it is too late; others we may never fully understand. We will never know, for instance, whether an extinct forest plant held the cure for cancer or AIDS. While scientists disagree on the causes and effects of deforestation, it is clear that forests are important natural resources that should not be wasted.

What Are the Consequences of Deforestation?

Primary Source Quotes

66 **Logging and road building destroy natural habitats, killing species, which disrupts the entire forest food chain.** 99

—Leonardo DiCaprio, *The 11th Hour.* Warner Independent Pictures, 2007. wip.warnerbros.com.

DiCaprio produced and narrated *The 11th Hour*, a documentary that describes the last moment when change is still possible.

66 **To the best of our scientific knowledge, no species has become extinct due to forestry.** 99

—Patrick Moore, "Green Guru Sees the Good for the Tree," *Age*, December 16, 2006.

Moore is an outspoken advocate of sustainable forestry and the chair and chief scientist of Greenspirit, a consultancy focusing on environmental policy and communications in natural resources, biodiversity, energy, and climate change.

Bracketed quotes indicate conflicting positions.

* Editor's Note: While the definition of a primary source can be narrowly or broadly defined, for the purposes of Compact Research, a primary source consists of: 1) results of original research presented by an organization or researcher; 2) eyewitness accounts of events, personal experience, or work experience; 3) first-person editorials offering pundits' opinions; 4) government officials presenting political plans and/or policies; 5) representatives of organizations presenting testimony or policy.

❝ It seems that the waters are rising higher now than in the past. The rains used to be very predictable but now the system is mixed up. We have rains falling during the wrong time of year. . . . The climate seems to be changing and it is affecting us. ❞

—Amasina, "An Interview with Amasina," Mongabay.com, July 28, 2008.

Amasina is a shaman in the Suriname rain forest near Brazil.

❝ Several interesting recent studies challenge conventional views on the relationship between forests and water. More trees may not always result in more water for humans, and fewer trees may not result in catastrophic floods. ❞

—The Food and Agriculture Organization of the United Nations, *State of the World's Forests 2007*.

The Food and Agriculture Organization collects, compiles, and analyzes data on a wide range of forest-related issues.

❝ If we lose forests, we lose the fight against climate change. ❞

—Forests Now Declaration, September 12, 2007.

In 2007 hundreds of people from across the world joined in calling for urgent action to protect tropical forests by signing the Forest Now Declaration.

❝ We need to constantly remind the people that deforestation is killing our planet. If all wars on this earth stop today, there would still be no hope for human beings if they continue to cut down trees. ❞

—World Prout Assembly, "East Africa Deforestation Exacerbates Droughts, Floods," November 10, 2006. www.worldproutassembly.org.

The World Prout Assembly is a global nonprofit organization that fights injustice and the exploitation of minorities and other groups of people.

> 66 The world's remaining tropical forests must be protected, because without them not only will the global climate not be stabilized, but the entire world will suffer. 99

—Wangari Maathai, at a luncheon hosted by the Avoided Deforestation Partners, New York City, September 22, 2008.

Maathai is a Kenyan political and environmental activist and winner of the 2004 Nobel Peace Prize.

> 66 The fact is that people in rural areas, particularly the poorest, are often very reliant on forests and trees to provide for their basic human needs and to keep them from sinking deeper into poverty. 99

—Pekka Patosaari, "Building Livelihoods and Assets for People and Forests," Forest Leadership Conference, March 1, 2005.

Patosaari is the director of the United Nations Forum on Forests.

> 66 Just as our lungs absorb carbon dioxide from the blood and infuse it with oxygen, green plants absorb carbon dioxide during photosynthesis and release oxygen into the atmosphere in return. Which is why forests are often referred to as the Earth's lungs. 99

—WWF, "The Importance of Forests," November 22, 2005. www.panda.org.

WWF is a global conservation organization that works on behalf of the environment.

> 66 The rain forests are not the 'lungs of the world.' This is total [garbage] in every sense. Stop and think a moment— what do lungs do? They take in oxygen and give out carbon dioxide. Just what we need. Well done, lads! 99

—Philip Stott, *Envirospin Watch*, May 20, 2005.

Stott is professor emeritus of biogeography at the School of Oriental and African Studies, University of London, and an editor of the *Journal of Biogeography*. Since retiring, Stott has had a series of blogs in which he monitors media coverage of environmental issues and science.

Facts and Illustrations

What Are the Consequences of Deforestation?

- Land covered with trees and other plants absorbs **20 times** as much rainwater as bare earth.

- Forest destruction around the world causes the loss of an estimated **500 billion tons** (446 billion metric tons) of topsoil every year.

- The WWF estimates that deforestation is responsible for **20 percent** of global greenhouse gas emissions; some scientists say this number is much higher.

- The World Conservation Union estimates that about **12.5 percent** of the world's 270,000 species of plants and about **75 percent** of the world's mammals are threatened by forest decline.

- Rain forests cover only **7 percent** of the land on Earth, but they contain nearly half of all the trees on Earth. A typical 2,500-acre (1,000 ha) patch of rain forest contains 1,500 species of flowering plants, 750 kinds of trees, 400 bird species, and more than 150 kinds of butterflies.

- Rain forests generate about **40 percent** of the world's oxygen and produce about **30 percent** of the planet's freshwater.

Forests Provide Many Ecosystem Services

Forests provide a wide range of benefits. The Millennium Ecosystem Assessment, an organization that assesses ecosystem change and what action should be taken to contribute to human well being, identified four basic categories of ecosystem services. The supporting services provided by forests, such as producing oxygen, rebuilding soils, and cycling nutrients, make possible all of the other services.

Ecosystem Services	
Supporting	**Provisioning**
	• Food
	• Freshwater
	• Wood and fiber
	• Fuel
	Regulating
• Nutrient cycling	• Climate regulation
• Soil formation	• Flood regulation
• Primary production	• Disease regulation
	• Water regulation
	Cultural
	• Aesthetic
	• Spiritual
	• Educational
	• Recreational

Source: The Millennium Assessment, Millennium Ecosystem Assessment Synthesis Report, 2005.

- Eighty to **90 percent** of people in developing countries rely on traditional medicine, based largely on plants. In the United States, roughly **25 percent** of prescriptions are filled with drugs whose active ingredients are extracted or derived from plants.

Where Trees Are at Risk

The number of threatened and endangered species is an indicator of the threat to biological diversity. The majority of vulnerable and endangered tree species are found in tropical forests. Trees provide critical habitat for many animals; the loss of tree species may thus contribute to greater extinction rates for animals.

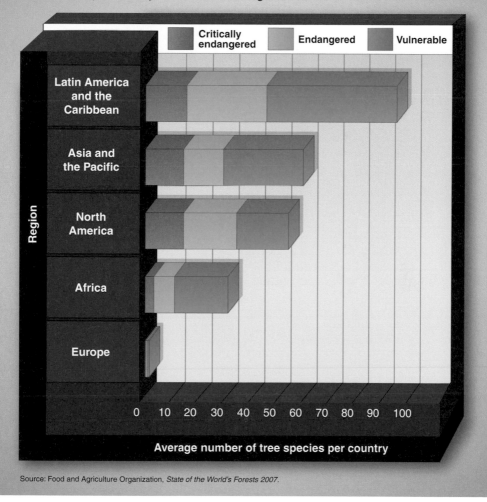

Source: Food and Agriculture Organization, *State of the World's Forests 2007.*

- Global carbon stocks in forest biomass decreased by about **5.5 percent** between 1990 and 2005.

10 Countries with the Largest Carbon Stocks (in Megatons)

One benefit of forests is their ability to sequester carbon, which many scientists and policy makers believe may be an answer to global warming. This chart shows the 10 countries with the largest carbon stocks from living biomass (dead materials were not included). Brazil, with almost 50,000 megatons of carbon (Mt C), provides far more carbon storage services than any other country.

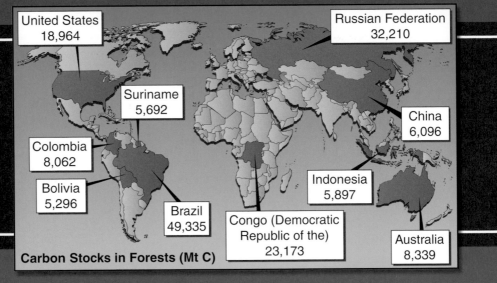

United States
18,964

Russian Federation
32,210

Suriname
5,692

China
6,096

Colombia
8,062

Bolivia
5,296

Indonesia
5,897

Brazil
49,335

Congo (Democratic Republic of the)
23,173

Australia
8,339

Carbon Stocks in Forests (Mt C)

Note: all numbers are in metric tons.

Source: United Nations Development Programme, "2007/2008 Human Development Report #24, Carbon Dioxide Emissions and Stocks," 2008.

- In many countries with temperate forests, there has been an **increase in carbon** stored in trees in recent years. This includes the United States, Canada, New Zealand, and Sweden.

- Experts suggest that failing to address deforestation could result in climate changes that will cost upward of **$1 trillion** a year by 2100.

How Can Deforestation Be Stopped?

66 If you are thinking a year ahead, sow a seed. If you are thinking ten years ahead, plant a tree. 99

—Chinese poet, circa 500 B.C.

66 Restoring forests involves much more than just planting new trees. It is also about restoring the goods and services that forests provide—improved water quality; soil stabilization; access to food, medicines and raw materials; and stable sources of income for local people. 99

—WWF, the global conservation organization.

Strategies for preserving forests operate on a local, national, or international scale. Some countries have done better in passing and enforcing forest protection laws than others have, causing many international policy, conservation, and activist groups to build broad coalitions to bring about change. On a local level, sustainable forest practices and reforestation may help to reverse deforestation trends. Many experts say that past policies have been overly focused on immediate causes of deforestation while neglecting the complex underlying causes, such as the impact of poverty and global inequities. In addition, consumers and other individuals, both near and far from the threatened forests, may play an important role in making sustainable choices.

Land Conservation

Many countries, including the United States, have historically set aside forested land for protection of biodiversity or soil and water resources. Public forests and other public lands are often managed for multiple uses, which means management strategies include wood production as well as the protection of species and ecological systems. In the United States and Canada, for instance, most commercial logging takes place on public lands. Worldwide, roughly 84 percent of forests are on public lands, but private ownership is on the rise.

> **In many countries the illegal trade in timber far exceeds the legal trade.**

In the past several years, many countries have increased the forest area designated for the conservation of biological diversity. From 1990 to 2005, the area designated for conservation worldwide expanded by 32 percent. Today over 11 percent of the world's forest areas have conservation as a primary goal. Another 300 million acres (121 million ha) are designated for soil and water conservation.

Regulation and Legislation

According to FAO, over 100 countries have national forest programs in place. Some of those with the most endangered forests have strengthened their protection measures in the past decade or so. Most countries in Africa adopted new, stronger forest policies and forest laws in the early 2000s.

Brazil has long been under attack by international conservation organizations for failing to do enough to protect the rich resources of the Amazon. The country's land tenure laws, for instance, give rights to people who are working the land, creating an incentive for people to clear new parts of the forest. On December 1, 2008, the Brazilian government announced a plan to cut deforestation of the Amazon by 70 percent over the next decade, marking the first time Brazil has set a target for reducing deforestation.

Law Enforcement

Even in countries with strict forest protection legislation, enforcement remains a problem. Although exact figures are difficult to determine, in many countries the illegal trade in timber far exceeds the legal trade. In Cambodia, for example, 90 percent of the harvest is thought to be illegal. In addition to the environmental damage, illegal operations promote corruption and cost governments billions of dollars.

Consumer countries contribute to these problems by importing timber and wood products without ensuring that they come from legal sources. A recent report from the WWF suggests that over one-quarter of the wood purchased by European countries was cut illegally.

Determining whether wood is from legal sources is sometimes more difficult than it appears. China buys half of the tropical logs traded internationally, and critics say that much of the wood is illegal. Chinese manufacturers use the wood in furniture and other items for export to the United States, Europe, and Japan.

Experts emphasize that it will take a concerted effort on the part of both producer and consumer countries to stop illegal logging. It may also require new funds. Many—if not most—poor countries lack adequate law enforcement resources to police large tracts of forest. The enforcement efforts of some countries are further hampered by corruption.

> " Among consumers . . . information about sustainable principles has increased the demand for wood products that have been produced and harvested in a sustainable manner. "

International Policy

A number of international organizations, most notably the United Nations, are working to address deforestation. In April 2007, for the first time countries adopted an agreement on international forest policy and cooperation. The United Nations reports, "The new agreement, although not legally binding, sets a standard in forest management that is expected to have a major impact on international cooperation and national action to reduce deforestation, prevent forest degradation, promote sustainable livelihoods and reduce poverty for all forest-dependent peoples."[36]

International cooperation is needed to increase value in the global marketplace for products that are certified as sustainably produced or harvested. Many international organizations also advocate paying poorer countries for the environmental benefits of their forests to discourage them from cutting down trees.

Conservation and Activism

The Nature Conservancy, Community Forestry International, the WWF, and Conservation International are among the many organizations working on a global scale to preserve forest resources and habitats. Some conservation organizations protect forests by purchasing large tracts of land. Others engage in global tree-planting efforts. Since it began in 1977, Kenya's Green Belt Movement has planted 40 million trees in that country. Inspired by the success of this organization, the United Nations Environment Programme initiated the Billion Tree Campaign, a worldwide effort to plant 1 billion trees each year.

> **Forest management goes beyond thinking of forests as a source of goods to consider the many other benefits forests provide, both to local populations and to the wider world.**

Among the most important roles of these nonprofit organizations is focusing attention on the causes and effects of deforestation. Activists work to bring attention to the state of the world's forests and encourage individual action. Among consumers, for instance, information about sustainable principles has increased the demand for wood products that have been produced and harvested in a sustainable manner. This in turn has contributed to a growing interest on the part of forestland owners and industries to engage in sustainable forest management and harvesting practices.

A continuum of tools for advancing sustainable forest management is available to policy makers and forest managers. On a local scale, governments work with forest communities to encourage low-impact agricultural activities and sustainable harvesting of wood and nonwood forest products. In some countries, such as Canada and Finland, the logging and pulp and paper industries systematically replace trees as they are harvested, often planting several trees for each one cut down.

Forest conservation advocates demonstrate how sustainable harvesting practices can be profitable. Sustainable forest management is further supported by programs that offer clear criteria for sustainability and a means for identifying and certifying wood and other forest products that have been obtained in a sustainable manner.

> " Plantations are counted in official forestry numbers, but they do not provide the same benefits as other types of forests. "

Forest management goes beyond thinking of forests as a source of goods to consider the many other benefits forests provide, both to local populations and to the wider world. Management techniques focus on maintaining a healthy ecosystem not only to protect trees and other forest resources but also to protect biodiversity. This so-called multiple-use approach includes appreciating forests as an aesthetic, cultural, and recreational resource.

Reforestation

If forestlands are left alone for long enough, trees and other life will regrow. The time needed for this natural reforestation process depends on the type of forest and the extent of the damage to the ecosystem resulting from deforestation. In the eastern United States, for instance, forested acreage is increasing due to the natural expansion and growth of forests that had once been cleared.

Many countries have programs to help reforest barren lands through managed reforestation programs. China, which has denuded most of its forests, has embarked on the largest reforestation project to date. Over a 10-year period ending in 2012, the country plans to plant 170,000 square miles (440,298 sq. km.) of trees—an area roughly the size of California.

Some scientists maintain that, since deforestation results in the extinction of plant and animal species, reforestation is not an answer. Still, recent studies suggest that a forest's ecological balance may be restored more quickly than previously thought. Reviewing the results of a program in which saplings were planted on desolate cattle pastures in Costa Rica's rain forests, scientists expressed optimism. "I'm surprised," said Carl Leopold, a scientist with the Boyce Thomson Institute for Plant Sciences. "We're getting impressive growth rates in the new forest trees."[37]

Tree Plantations

Tree plantations are groves of trees planted for harvest. Some plantations are grown by state forestry authorities; others are planted by private corporations. In southern and southeastern Asia, there are a growing number of rubber and oil palm plantations; some Asian countries are also experimenting with teak plantations.

Plantations are counted in official forestry numbers, but they do not provide the same benefits as other types of forests. Plantations are usually monocultures, with the same species of tree planted in a large area. In addition, the trees in plantations are harvested as soon as they are mature—after just 10 years for some species.

> Buying recycled paper, shade-grown coffee, and products made from certified woods are just a few of the ways that consumers can encourage sustainable forestry practices.

Although plantation forests do not offer all of the ecological services of old-growth forests, advocates emphasize that by meeting the demand for wood they may reduce future deforestation. Some calculations indicate that harvesting trees on plantations requires far less land than harvesting the same trees in natural forests, thereby providing more room for other land uses, including natural forests.

Getting the Word Out

One of the best ways to protect the forest may be to improve awareness. As one author says, "Until more people know about the threats, the trees will continue to fall."[38] To this end, many celebrities—Leonardo DiCaprio, Naomi Campbell, William Shatner—have used their fame to raise awareness. Some people have taken activism a step further. In 1989, for instance, Sting and his wife, Trudie Styler, formed the Rainforest Foundation "after witnessing firsthand the destruction of the Amazon rainforest."[39] The Rainforest Foundation works with indigenous populations in protection efforts.

For those who would like to take a stand by refusing to purchase wood from tropical rain forests, it can be nearly impossible to identify which products come from these forests and which are from sustainable forests. Various organizations, such as the Forest Stewardship Council, have developed certifying procedures based on standards that encourage the use of wood from sustainable forests.

What Individuals Can Do

Many conservation organizations emphasize that the future of the forests lies in the hands of regular people. They advocate "going green." Buying recycled paper, shade-grown coffee, and products made from certified woods are just a few of the ways that consumers can encourage sustainable forestry practices. Some organizations also suggest boycotting products unsustainably grown in rain forests and/or from countries that lack adequate protection for their forests. Some people even suggest that not eating beef may reduce the demand for cattle ranching in Latin America.

Some forest advocates suggest that these measures may have little impact, since they do little to help alleviate the underlying causes of deforestation. In fact, say some people, refusing to purchase goods from some countries may increase the poverty of the people living there, making it more likely those people will exploit forest resources.

A Complex Solution for a Complex Problem

Deforestation has many causes. Thus, it must be addressed through decisive action on a number of fronts. The best strategy is an approach that addresses both immediate and root causes. Passing laws will do little if countries lack the means to enforce the laws. Advocating the ecological need for protecting the forests will be unsuccessful if people are not given other ways to make a living. As Prince Charles said as he ushered in his rain forest project, "We have to ensure the forests are worth more alive than dead."[40]

How Can Deforestation Be Stopped?

> 66 Governments and organizations can improve their corporate social responsibility and lighten their environmental footprint through policies and procurement processes that encourage the use of wood and paper products from well-managed forests. 99

—Forest Products Association of Canada, "Tackle Climate Change: Use Wood," 2008. www.bcforestinformation.com.

Forest Products Association of Canada is the voice of Canada's wood, pulp, and paper producers.

> 66 The government should be promoting forest protection to tackle climate change, not logging. 99

—Chris Henschel, "Environmentalists Decry BC Government's Exclusive Focus on Using Wood as Forest Climate Strategy," press release, ForestEthics, September 25, 2008. www.forestethics.org.

Henschel is the national manager of conservation and climate at the Canadian Parks and Wilderness Society.

Bracketed quotes indicate conflicting positions.

* Editor's Note: While the definition of a primary source can be narrowly or broadly defined, for the purposes of Compact Research, a primary source consists of: 1) results of original research presented by an organization or researcher; 2) eyewitness accounts of events, personal experience, or work experience; 3) first-person editorials offering pundits' opinions; 4) government officials presenting political plans and/or policies; 5) representatives of organizations presenting testimony or policy.

66 The energy challenges our country faces are severe and have gone unaddressed for far too long. Our addiction to foreign oil doesn't just undermine our national security and wreak havoc on our environment—it cripples our economy and strains the budgets of working families all across America. 99

—The White House, "The Agenda: Energy and the Environment," January 2009. www.whitehouse.gov.

The White House Web site presents the Obama administration's positions on energy and many other issues.

66 Sustainable forest management is more than just growing and protecting trees—it is highly complex and can only be addressed through a range of actions that blend technical aspects of forestry with other considerations such as how to strengthen policy and governance frameworks to engaging market actors and mobilizing the necessary resources. 99

—Warren Evans, "World Bank Develops Practical Guidance for Sustaining Forests in Development Cooperation," press release, February 26, 2008.

Evans is the director for environment at the World Bank.

66 The arrival of the timber industry is often the first kiss of death for intact rainforests. Much has been said about making the tropical timber industry 'sustainable' and forest-friendly. But in reality, this has never happened and may not even be possible due to the complex ecology of tropical forests. 99

—Simon Counsell, The Rainforest Foundation Annual Review: 2006–2007. www.rainforestfoundationuk.org.

Counsell is the executive director of the Rainforest Foundation.

66 Conventional wisdom suggests that forest benefits are undervalued by markets; the question is what to do about it. **99**

—The Food and Agriculture Organization of the United Nations, *State of the World's Forests 2007*.

The Food and Agriculture Organization collects, compiles, and analyzes data on a wide range of forest-related issues.

66 Allowing people in forested regions of developing countries to participate in carbon markets presents major challenges, but it's naive to think that conservation is going to occur absent a market incentive. **99**

—Meine van Noordwijk, "Report Finds Deforestation Offers Very Little Money Compared to Potential Financial Benefits," World Agroforestry Centre, November 2007. www.worldagroforestry.org.

Van Noordwijk is the Southeast Asia regional coordinator of the World Agroforestry Centre.

66 Using wood sends a signal to the marketplace to grow more trees and to produce more wood. That means we can then use less concrete, steel and plastic—heavy carbon emitters through their production. Trees are the only abundant, biodegradable and renewable global resource. **99**

—Patrick Moore, "An Inconvenient Fact," *Vancouver (BC) Sun*, August 29, 2007.

Moore is an outspoken advocate of sustainable forestry and the chairman and chief scientist of Greenspirit, a consultancy focusing on environmental policy and communications in natural resources, biodiversity, energy, and climate change.

How Can Deforestation Be Stopped?

- Several countries, including Brazil, the Philippines, Thailand, and India, have declared deforestation a **national emergency**.

- According to the World Bank, more than **25 percent** of the world's population—an estimated 1.6 billion people—rely on forest resources for their livelihoods; **90 percent** of these people—almost 1.2 billion—live in **extreme poverty**.

- In 2005 over 1 billion acres (405 million ha)—roughly **11 percent** of the world's forests—were designated for conservation. From 1990 to 2005, the area so designated increased by **32 percent**, a total increase of over 237 million acres (96 million ha).

- The area of productive forest plantations increased by **6.2 million acres** (2.5 million ha) between 2000 and 2005. Forests planted for production and for protective purposes are both steadily increasing in all regions except Africa.

- An estimated **20 to 27 percent** of the wood products imported by European countries is illegally harvested.

- In many countries the illegal trade in timber far exceeds the legal trade. Ninety percent of the harvest in Cambodia is thought to be illegal; **80 percent** in Bolivia, Peru, and the Brazilian Amazon; and **75 percent** in Indonesia.

Where Illegal Logging Is a Problem

In some countries the trade of illegally procured wood and wood products exceeds the legal market. Experts indicate that illegal logging not only robs governments of millions of dollars, it also can be a major contributor to deforestation. The following chart shows some of the countries in which illegal logging is a problem.

Country	Estimated Illegal Logging as Percent of Production
Africa	
Benin	80 percent
Cameroon	50 percent
Ghana	At least 66 percent
Mozambique	50–70 percent
Asia	
Cambodia	90 percent
Indonesia	Up to 66–88 percent
Malaysia	Up to 33 percent
Myanmar	80 percent
Latin America	
Bolivia	80 percent
Brazil	80 percent in the Amazon
Colombia	42 percent
Ecuador	70 percent
Honduras	75–85 percent of hardwood 30–50 percent of softwood
Nicaragua	40–45 percent
Costa Rica	25 percent
Europe and North Asia	
Albania	90 percent
Azerbaijan	Very large
Bulgaria	45 percent
Georgia	85 percent
Russia	20–40 percent

Source: Paris: Round Table on Sustainable Development, "The Economics of Illegal Logging and Associated Trade," January 2007.

Conservation Lands

An increasing number of countries are taking steps to conserve forestlands. Globally, more than 11 percent of the total forest has been designated primarily for conservation of biological diversity. This bar graph shows that Africa—with over 16 percent of its forests designated for conservation—leads the world in this category, followed closely by the Near East and Asia.

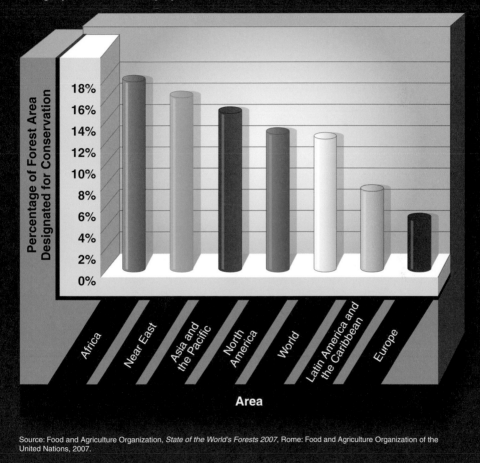

Source: Food and Agriculture Organization, *State of the World's Forests 2007*, Rome: Food and Agriculture Organization of the United Nations, 2007.

- Almost **50 percent** of the total new wood produced worldwide comes from planted forests.

The Rapid Growth of Protected Areas in the Tropics

One of the more common methods of addressing deforestation is to set aside forested areas as protected land. This figure shows the growth of various types of protected lands. Although many protected lands are underfunded and lack the ongoing management that is critical to their success, studies suggest that designating land as a protected area does in fact deter deforestation.

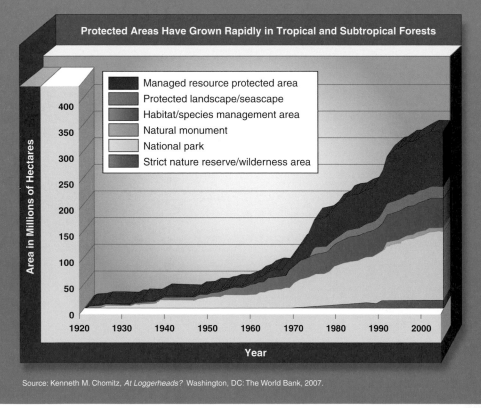

Protected Areas Have Grown Rapidly in Tropical and Subtropical Forests

Legend:
- Managed resource protected area
- Protected landscape/seascape
- Habitat/species management area
- Natural monument
- National park
- Strict nature reserve/wilderness area

Y-axis: Area in Millions of Hectares (0, 50, 100, 150, 200, 250, 300, 350, 400)

X-axis: Year (1920, 1930, 1940, 1950, 1960, 1970, 1980, 1990, 2000)

Source: Kenneth M. Chomitz, *At Loggerheads?* Washington, DC: The World Bank, 2007.

- The average American uses over 700 pounds (318 kg) of paper each year—more than **90 percent** of the printing and writing paper used in the United States is made from virgin tree fiber.

- To make up for the loss of trees in the past decade, people would need to plant over **300 million acres** (121 million ha)—an area the size of Peru.

Carbon Financing

Many policy makers have proposed paying nations for the environmental benefits provided by their forests. Proposals put a dollar value on the carbon storage provided by forests of selected nations. The payments could be worth billions of dollars to some of the world's poorest and most indebted countries. This chart demonstrates the percentage increase in per capita income that could result from this approach, based on current deforestation rates and a high price per ton of carbon ($20 U.S.).

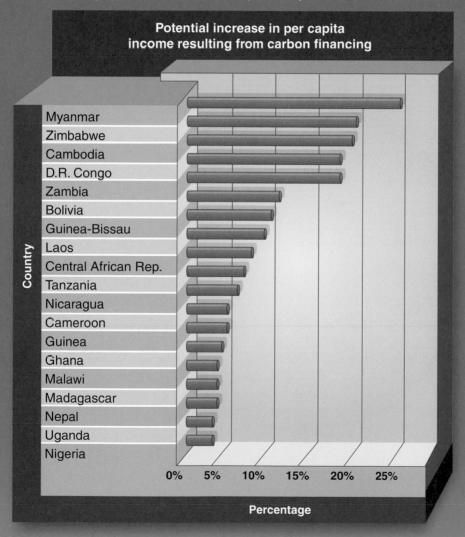

Potential increase in per capita income resulting from carbon financing

Countries listed (top to bottom): Myanmar, Zimbabwe, Cambodia, D.R. Congo, Zambia, Bolivia, Guinea-Bissau, Laos, Central African Rep., Tanzania, Nicaragua, Cameroon, Guinea, Ghana, Malawi, Madagascar, Nepal, Uganda, Nigeria

Y-axis: Country
X-axis: Percentage (0%, 5%, 10%, 15%, 20%, 25%)

Source: Rhett A. Butler, "Avoided Deforestation Could Help Fight Third World Poverty Under Global Warming Pact," mongabay.com. October 31, 2006.

Key People and Advocacy Groups

Avoided Deforestation Partners (ADP): ADP is an international network of thinkers and strategists, founded in May 2007 by leaders in carbon policy, finance, forestry, and conservation to support international efforts to halt tropical deforestation. ADP promotes the adoption of a policy framework that creates mechanisms to encourage investments to avoid further deforestation.

Al Gore: Former vice president Gore is an outspoken advocate for addressing deforestation as part of the fight against global warming. He won the 2007 Nobel Peace Prize for his efforts to build awareness about human-induced climate change.

Jeff Horowitz: Horowitz is the founder and president of Avoided Deforestation Partners, which offers market-driven solutions to address deforestation. Among the methods ADP recommends is using carbon credits to reimburse poor countries for protecting forests from being converted to other uses.

David Kaimowitz: Currently the director general for the Center for International Forestry Research, Kaimowitz is one of the world's most respected scientists and observers in international forestry.

Wangari Maathai: Maathai is a Kenyan political and environmental activist. She is best known for founding the Green Belt Movement, which, since its inception in 1977, has planted more than 40 million trees in Kenya. In 2004 Maathai became the first African woman to receive the Nobel Peace Prize.

Patrick Moore: Moore, a founding member of Greenpeace, is among the most outspoken critics of current approaches taken by environmentalists to save forests. In 1991 Moore founded Greenspirit, a consultancy focusing on environmental policy and communications in natural resources, biodiversity, energy, and climate change.

Norman Myers: Myers is a renowned biologist and expert on deforestation and the extinction of species. He is currently a fellow at the University of Oxford in England.

Pekka Patosaari: As the director of the United Nations Forum on Forests, Patosaari is an international spokesperson for the sustainable management and protection of the world's forests.

Prince Charles: Charles, Prince of Wales, speaks out on the global need to address climate change. He established the Prince's Rainforests Project in 2007 to raise awareness of deforestation.

Rainforest Action Network (RAN): RAN is an activist organization that works to preserve the world's rain forests by addressing issues such as the logging and importation of timber, cattle ranching, and the rights of indigenous people in rain forests. It also seeks to educate the public about the environmental effects of harvesting tropical hardwoods.

Sting: The international rock superstar has worked on behalf of rain forests for over two decades. In 1989 he founded the Rainforest Foundation with his wife, Trudie Styler. Sting also hosts an annual concert to raise money to protect the world's rain forests.

WWF: WWF—the World Wildlife Fund in the United States and the Worldwide Fund for Nature in all other countries—is the world's largest conservation organization. It engages in a wide range of activities to protect the environment and the diversity and abundance of life on Earth.

Chronology

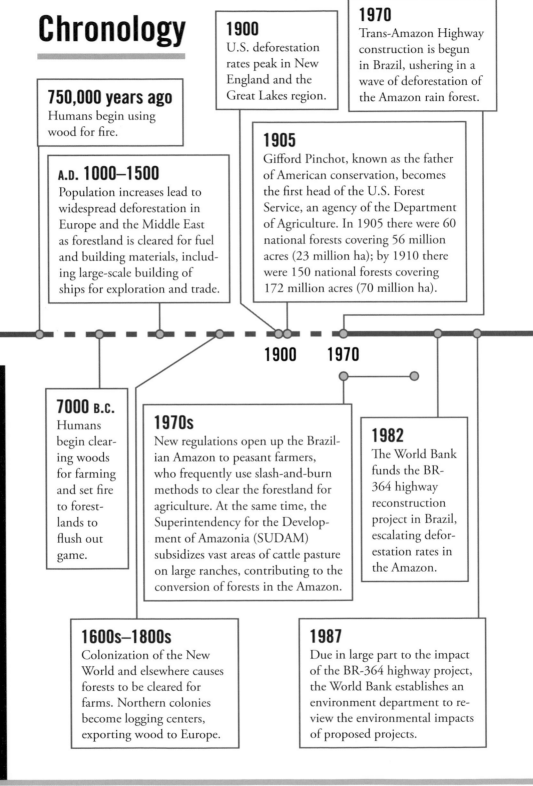

750,000 years ago
Humans begin using wood for fire.

A.D. 1000–1500
Population increases lead to widespread deforestation in Europe and the Middle East as forestland is cleared for fuel and building materials, including large-scale building of ships for exploration and trade.

1900
U.S. deforestation rates peak in New England and the Great Lakes region.

1970
Trans-Amazon Highway construction is begun in Brazil, ushering in a wave of deforestation of the Amazon rain forest.

1905
Gifford Pinchot, known as the father of American conservation, becomes the first head of the U.S. Forest Service, an agency of the Department of Agriculture. In 1905 there were 60 national forests covering 56 million acres (23 million ha); by 1910 there were 150 national forests covering 172 million acres (70 million ha).

1900   1970

7000 B.C.
Humans begin clearing woods for farming and set fire to forestlands to flush out game.

1970s
New regulations open up the Brazilian Amazon to peasant farmers, who frequently use slash-and-burn methods to clear the forestland for agriculture. At the same time, the Superintendency for the Development of Amazonia (SUDAM) subsidizes vast areas of cattle pasture on large ranches, contributing to the conversion of forests in the Amazon.

1982
The World Bank funds the BR-364 highway reconstruction project in Brazil, escalating deforestation rates in the Amazon.

1600s–1800s
Colonization of the New World and elsewhere causes forests to be cleared for farms. Northern colonies become logging centers, exporting wood to Europe.

1987
Due in large part to the impact of the BR-364 highway project, the World Bank establishes an environment department to review the environmental impacts of proposed projects.

1988
Chico Mendes, activist and rubber trapper, is assassinated by a rancher in Brazil, increasing international attention to Amazonian deforestation.

1997
The Kyoto Protocol is signed, legally binding countries to take steps to address climate change. Deforestation is not included in the provisions.

1992
The United Nations Conference on Environment and Development (UNCED), better known as the Earth Summit, is held in Rio de Janeiro. Conventions on climate and biodiversity are signed.

2007
At the United Nations, countries adopt an agreement on international forest policy and cooperation for the first time, and hundreds of people sign the Forest Now Declaration, calling for urgent action to protect tropical forests.

1990

2000

1999
"An Emergency Call to Action for the Forests and Their Peoples" petition is presented to the United Nations, calling for immediate steps to stop deforestation.

2004
A tsunami hits 13 countries in Southeast Asia, killing more than 300,000 people. Some scientists believe the deforestation of coastal mangrove forests contributed to the damage.

1993
The Forest Stewardship Council (FSC) is established as an international nonprofit organization that promotes stewardship of the planet's forests. The FSC certifies products that support responsible forest management.

2005
Dorothy Stang, a nun and environmental activist who spoke out against deforestation and criminal gangs who stole property from peasant farmers, is killed by gunslingers who had been hired by ranchers.

2008
The annual rate of deforestation in Brazil's Amazon forests increases for the first time in many years, causing environmentalists to demand that Brazil adopt a zero deforestation policy.

Related Organizations

Center for International Forestry Research (CIFOR)

PO Box 0113

BOCBD

Bogor 16000, Indonesia

phone: +62-251-8622-622 • fax: +62-251-8622-100

e-mail: cifor@cgiar.org • Web site: www.cifor.cgiar.org

CIFOR is an international forestry research organization that works through research partnerships to take a holistic, interdisciplinary approach to solving forest-related problems with the aim of contributing to the sustainable well-being of people in developing countries, particularly in the tropics.

Environmental Defense Fund

257 Park Ave. South

New York, NY 10010

phone: (212) 505-2100 • fax: (212) 505-0892

Web site: www.edf.org

Founded in 1967, this nonprofit organization of scientists, lawyers, and economists is dedicated to protecting the environmental rights of all people, including future generations.

Food and Agriculture Organization of the United Nations (FAO)

Forestry Department

Viale delle Terme di Caracalla

00153 Rome, Italy

phone: +39-06-57051 • fax: +39-06-57053152

e-mail: fao-hq@fao.org • Web site: www.fao.org

The FAO Forestry Department helps nations manage their forests in a sustainable way. FAO offers direct technical support, brings countries together to discuss technical and policy issues related to forests, and provides a wealth of information on forests and forest management. Among its activities, the FAO collects, analyzes, and disseminates forest data that include the extent and rate of deforestation.

Forest Stewardship Council (FSC)

212 Third Ave. North, Suite 280

Minneapolis, MN 55401

phone: (612) 353-4511 • fax: (612) 208-1565

e-mail: info@fscus.org • Web site: www.fscus.org

The FSC was created by loggers, foresters, environmentalists, and sociologists in 1993. The FSC sets forth principles, criteria, and standards that span economic, social, and environmental concerns. The U.S. branch promotes FSC certification for sustainable management practices.

Global Canopy Programme

John Krebs Field Station

Wytham

Oxford OX2 8QJ

United Kingdom

phone: +44 (0) 1865 724 333 • fax: +44 (0) 1865 724 555

Web site: www.globalcanopy.org

Established in 2001, the Global Canopy Programme is an international alliance linking 38 leading institutions in 19 countries engaged in research, education, and conservation efforts investigating the impact of climate change on biodiversity and ecosystem services maintained by forest canopies.

Rainforest Foundation US

32 Broadway, Suite 1614

New York, NY 10004

phone: 212-431-9098 • fax: 212-431-9197

e-mail: rffny@rffny.org • Web site: www.rainforestfoundation.org

Founded in 1989 by Sting and his wife, Trudie Styler, to address deforestation issues in the Amazon, the mission and scope of the Rainforest

Foundation has expanded. Today there are three autonomous Rainforest Foundation organizations (in addition to the Rainforest US, there is the Rainforest UK and Rainforest Norway) that have projects in more than a dozen countries. Each of these organizations raises money and awareness to address deforestation issues and help the plight of the indigenous peoples in rain forest areas.

United Nations Environment Programme (UNEP)

UNEP Regional Office for North America

900 Seventeenth St. NW, Suite 506

Washington, DC 20006

phone: (202) 785-0465 • fax: (202) 785-2096

Web site: www.unep.org

The goal of UNEP is to provide leadership and encourage partnership in caring for the environment by inspiring, informing, and enabling nations and peoples to improve their quality of life without compromising that of future generations. Among the programs of interest is the Billion Tree Campaign, a worldwide effort to plant 1 billion trees each year.

United Nations Forum on Forests (UNFF)

The United Nations Forum on Forests Secretariat

DC1-1245

One UN Plaza

New York, NY 10017

phone: (212) 963-3401 • fax: (917) 367-3186

Web site: www.un.org/esa/forests

The UNFF is a subsidiary body of the United Nations that was formed in 2000 to promote conservation and sustainable development of forests. The UNFF serves as an international forum for international policy making and offers a wealth of information on forestry issues.

World Agroforestry Centre

United Nations Avenue, Gigiri

PO Box 30677-00100 GPO

Nairobi, Kenya

phone: +254-20-722-4000; or (650) 833-6645 (U.S.)

fax: +254-20-722-4001; or (650) 833-6646 (U.S.)

e-mail: icraf@cgiar.org • Web site: www.worldagroforestrycentre.org

The mission of the World Agroforestry Centre is to generate science-based knowledge about the diverse roles that trees play in agricultural landscapes and to use its research to advance policies and practices that benefit the poor and the environment.

World Rainforest Movement

Ricardo Carrere

Maldonado 1858

Montevideo 11200, Uruguay

phone: 598-2-413-2989 • fax: 598-2-410-0985

e-mail: wrm@wrm.org.uy • Web site: www.wrm.org.uy

The World Rainforest Movement is an international network of citizens' groups involved in efforts to defend the world's forests.

WWF

WWF United States

1250 Twenty-fourth St. NW

Washington, DC

phone: (202) 293-4800 • fax: (202) 293-9211

Web site: www.worldwildlife.org, or www.panda.org (U.S.)

WWF—the World Wildlife Fund in the United States and the World-wide Fund for Nature in all other countries—is the world's largest conservation organization, working in 100 countries for nearly half a century. With the support of almost 5 million members worldwide, WWF is dedicated to delivering science-based solutions to preserve the diversity and abundance of life on Earth, stop the degradation of the environment, and combat climate change.

For Further Research

Books

Michael Allaby, *Biomes of the Earth: Tropical Forests*. New York: Chelsea House, 2006.

Lester R. Brown, *Plan B: Rescuing a Planet Under Stress and a Civilization in Trouble*. New York: Norton, 2003.

Kenneth M. Chomitz, *At Loggerheads? Agricultural Expansion, Poverty Reduction and Environment in the Tropical Forest*. Washington, DC: World Bank, 2007.

Collins UK Staff, *Fragile Earth: Views of a Changing World*. New York: HarperCollins, 2006.

Helen Cothran, ed., *Global Resources: Opposing Viewpoints*. Detroit: Greenhaven, 2003.

Douglas Dupler, ed., *Conserving the Environment: Opposing Viewpoints*. Detroit: Greenhaven, 2006.

Yadvinder Malhi and Oliver Phillips, *Tropical Forests and Global Atmospheric Change*. Cambridge, England: Oxford University Press, 2005.

Sergio Margulis, *Causes of Deforestation of the Brazilian Amazon*. Washington, DC: World Bank, 2003.

Sharon L. Spray and Matthew D. Moran, eds., *Tropical Deforestation*. Lanham, MD: Rowman & Littlefield, 2006.

Michael Williams, *Deforesting the Earth: From Prehistory to Global Crisis*. Abridged ed. Chicago: University of Chicago Press, 2006.

Charles H. Wood and Roberto Porro, eds., *Deforestation and Land Use in the Amazon*. Gainesville: University Press of Florida, 2002.

Periodicals and Internet Sources

BBC, "Brazil Amazon Deforestation Soars," January 24, 2008. http://news.bbc.co.uk/2/hi/americas/7206165.stm.

————, "Deforestation and the Greenhouse Effect," March 4, 2008. www.bbc.co.uk/dna/h2g2/A3556848.

Peter Bunyard, "Crisis? What Crisis? Amazon Rainforest Damage Assessments Conflict," *Ecologist*, October 2000. http://findarticles.com/p/articles/mi_m2465/is_7_30/ai_66457060?tag=content;col1.

Rhett A. Butler, "An Interview with Ethnobotanist Dr. Mark Plotkin," Mongabay.com, October 31, 2006. http://news.mongabay.com/2006/1031-interview_plotkin.html.

————, "Tropical Rainforests: Imperiled Riches—Threatened Rainforests," Mongabay.com, January 9, 2006. http://rainforests.mongabay.com/0807.htm.

Carbonfund.org, "Reforestation." www.carbonfund.org.

Raymond Colitt, "Brazil Indians, Activists Protest over Amazon Dam," Reuters, May 21, 2008. www.reuters.com/article/americasCrisis/idU SN21415214.

FAO Forestry Department, *Global Forest Resources Assessment 2005*. Rome: United Nations Food and Agriculture Organization, 2005.

————, *State of the World's Forests 2007*. Rome: United Nations Food and Agriculture Organization, 2007.

Raffi Khatchadourian, "The Stolen Forests: Inside the Covert War on Illegal Logging," *New Yorker*, October 6, 2008. www.newyorker.com/reporting/2008/10/06/081006fa_fact_khatchadourian.

Nicholas D. Kristof, "Can We Be as Smart as Bats?" *New York Times*, May 1, 2008. www.nytimes.com/2008/05/01/opinion/01kristof.html.

Rebecca Lindsey, "Tropical Deforestation," *Earth Observatory*, NASA, March 30, 2007. http://earthobservatory.nasa.gov/Library/Deforest ation.

National Geographic, "Eye in the Sky: Deforestation and Desertification." www.nationalgeographic.com/eye/deforestation/deforestation. html.

Carlos Nobre, Myanna Lahsen, and Jean Ometto, "A Scientific and Technological Revolution for the Amazon," *Global Change Newsletter*, May 2008.

Real Truth, "Amazon Deforestation Rate Escalates," February 7, 2008. www.realtruth.org/news/080207-001-weather.html.

Elizabeth Rosenthal, "Once a Dream Fuel, Palm Oil May Be an Eco-Nightmare," *New York Times*, January 31, 2007. www.nytimes.com/2007/01/31/business/worldbusiness/31biofuel.html.

United Nations Environment Programme, The Billion Tree Campaign Site, "Facts and Figures." www.unep.org/billiontreecampaign/Facts Figures/QandA/index.asp.

USA Today, "Deforestation Exacerbates Haiti Floods," September 23, 2004. www.usatoday.com/weather/hurricane/2004-09-23-haiti-defo rest_x.htm.

Wild Again, "Facts and Figures." www.wild-again.org/UKsite/Facts-And-Figures-UK.html.

WWF, "Forests." www.worldwildlife.org/what/globalmarkets/forests/in dex.html.

Source Notes

Overview

1. FAO, "Definitional Issues Related to Reducing Emissions Due to Deforestation," *Forests and Climate Change Working Paper 5*. Rome: FAO, 2007. www.fao.org.
2. World Rainforest Movement, "The Direct and Underlying Causes of Forest Loss," WRM Briefing. www.wrm.org.uy.
3. Quoted in Mongabay.com, "Africa's Deforestation Rate May Be Underestimated," June 22, 2006. http://news.mongabay.com.
4. Bjørn Lomborg, *The Skeptical Environmentalist: Measuring the Real State of the World*. Cambridge, UK: Cambridge University Press, 2001.
5. Quoted in Barry Wigmore, "Rainforest Sting," *Range*, April 3, 2005. www.rangemagazine.com.
6. Raffi Khatchadourian, "The Stolen Forests: Inside the Covert War on Illegal Logging," *New Yorker*, October 6, 2008, p. 4. www.newyorker.com.
7. Greenpeace, "Indigenous Peoples and Ancient Forests," press backgrounder, October 1999. http://archive.greenpeace.org.
8. Avoided Deforestation Partners, "Why Communities?" AvoidedDeforestationPartners.org. www.adpartners.org.
9. Rebecca Lindsey, "Tropical Deforestation," *Earth Observatory*, March 30, 2007, p. 25.

How Serious Is Deforestation?

10. National Geographic, "Deforestation." http://environment.nationalgeographic.com.
11. FAO Forestry Department, *Global Forest Resources Assessment 2005*. Rome: United Nations Food and Agriculture Organization, 2005, p. 161.
12. FAO Forestry Department, *Global Forest Resources Assessment 2005*, p. xii.
13. Quoted in *ScienceDaily*, "The Future of Tropical Forest Species: New Projections Hopeful," April 8, 2006. www.sciencedaily.com.
14. Quoted in Global Change Program at the University of Michigan, "Global Deforestation," lecture, January 4, 2006. www.globalchange.umich.edu.
15. Scott Wallace, "Amazon Rain Forest," *National Geographic*, January 2007, p. 4. http://ngm.nationalgeographic.com.
16. Bjørn Lomborg, *The Skeptical Environmentalist: Measuring the Real State of the World*. Cambridge, UK: Cambridge University Press, 2001, p. 10.
17. Quoted in Alison Benjamin and Agencies, "More than Half of Amazon Will Be Lost by 2030, Report Warns," *Guardian*, December 6, 2007. www.guardian.co.uk.
18. Quoted in Greenpeace Southeast Asia, "Greenpeace Calls on Indonesian Citizens to Take Action to Safeguard the Nation's Forests as Esperanza Arrives in Manokwari," press release, October 17, 2008. www.greenpeace.org.
19. Rhett A. Butler, "Goodbye to West Africa's Rainforests," Mongabay.com, January 22, 2006. http://news.mongabay.com.

What Causes Deforestation?

20. World Rainforest Movement, "The Direct and Underlying Causes of Forest Loss." www.wrm.org.uy.

21. FAO, "Cattle Ranching and Deforestation," Livestock Policy Brief 03, p. 1. ftp://ftp.fao.org.

22. Patrick Moore, "Key Environmental Issues," Greenspirit, p. 3. www.greenspirit.com.

23. WWF, "Oil and Gas Extraction in the Amazon," October 21, 2008. www.panda.org.

24. Frederick A.B. Meyerson, "Population Growth and Deforestation: A Critical and Complex Relationship," Population Reference Bureau, June 2004. www.prb.org.

25. Rhett A. Butler, "Population and Poverty," Mongabay.com. http://rainforests.mongabay.com.

What Are the Consequences of Deforestation?

26. "Adaptations of Forest and Forest Management to Changing Climate with Emphasis on Forest Health: A Review of Science, Policies and Practices," Conference Report, Umea, Sweden, 2008, p. 2. www.forestadaptation2008.net.

27. Dan Shapley, "Java Landslide Death Toll Reaches 107: Deforestation Is a Root Cause of Human Devastation," *Daily Green*, January 2, 2008. www.thedailygreen.com.

28. Quoted in Jeremy Elton Jacquot, "Trees Are Nature's Natural Air Conditioners, Study Finds," *Treehugger*, November 1, 2008. www.treehugger.com.

29. NASA, "Tropical Deforestation Affects Rainfall in the U.S. and Around the Globe," September 13, 2005. www.nasa.gov.

30. Quoted in Barry Wigmore, "Rainforest Sting," *Range*, April 3, 2005. www.rangemagazine.com.

31. Reuters, "Nobel Peace Laureates Al Gore and Wangari Maathai Warn of Threat to National Security and Stability Without U.S. Leadership on Deforestation," press release, September 22, 2008. www.reuters.com.

32. Pekka Patosaari, "Building Livelihoods and Assets for People and Forests," paper presented at Forest Leadership Conference, Toronto, March 1, 2005.

33. Rebecca Lindsey, "Tropical Deforestation," *Earth Observatory*, NASA, March 30, 2007.

34. Peter Bunyard, "Crisis? What Crisis? *Ecologist*, October 2000, p. 56.

35. Rhett A. Butler, "An Interview with Amasina, a Shaman in the Amazon Rainforest," Mongabay.com, July 28, 2008. http://news.mongabay.com.

How Can Deforestation Be Stopped?

36. UN News Centre, "UN Adopts New International Agreement to Protect World's Forests," press release, April 28, 2007. www.un.org.

37. Quoted in *ScienceDaily*, "Restoration of a Tropical Rain Forest Ecosystem Successful on Small Scale," April 30, 2008. www.sciencedaily.com.

38. National Geographic Eye in the Sky, "Deforestation and Desertification: Toward a Greener Earth." www.nationalgeographic.com.

39. Rainforest Foundation UK, "In the Beginning." www.rainforestfoundationuk.org.

40. Quoted in Prince's Rainforests Project for Schools, "About the Project." www.princesrainforestsproject.org.

List of Illustrations

Index